NEW RETIREMENT RULES™

Strategies for Succeeding in The Coming Economic Collapse

Third Edition

By Dennis Tubbergen

New Retirement Rules™

Strategies for Succeeding in the Coming Economic Collapse

Third Edition

Published in the United States of America

by Dennis Tubbergen

TABLE OF CONTENTS

Introduction 5

Chapter One: The Problems with the Financial Industry 7

Chapter Two: What is Money? 23

Chapter Three: Predictable Economic Seasons 47

Chapter Four: Demographics 75

Chapter Five: Winter Season Investment Forecast 81

Chapter Six: How Asset Classes May Perform in Each Economic Season 97

Chapter Seven: Navigating and Prospering in the Economic Winter Season 105

Chapter Eight: The "Two bucket" Approach 119

Chapter Nine: Implementing the "Two Bucket" Approach in Your Situation 149

Introduction

You're likely reading this book to learn more about today's economy and to discover how to better manage your nest egg in the years ahead.

Let me congratulate you. The fact of the matter is, no one cares as much about your money as you do. Educating yourself and gaining multiple perspectives is the first step toward effective asset and investment management.

A few years ago, when I first wrote this book, I believed those undertaking retirement planning faced one of the most difficult planning environments ever. Today, despite what feels like a good economy, I am even more convinced that the planning environment will soon change significantly and become very difficult.

I have come to the conclusions outlined in this book after a decade of studying economic and financial history and conducting hundreds of interviews with very bright investing, economic, and financial minds.

The title of this book, *New Retirement Rules™: Strategies for Succeeding in the Coming Economic Collapse*, reflects my views of the inevitable outcome of today's economic conditions.

Parts of this book may shock you.

The premise of this book is that where we are headed, economically speaking, is predictable. Economic cycles and money cycles have existed for 2,500 years. I have concluded from my study of economic history that where we are today, economically speaking, and where we go from here are as predictable as the sun rising and setting each day.

Economic and money cycles are predictable because the collective behavior of humans is predictable. Faced with the same set of facts and circumstances, groups of humans tend to behave as groups of humans before them faced with the same circumstances.

Even more predictable is the collective behavior of groups of politicians.

Other parts of this book may anger you.

From my experience, most rendering advice to clients in the financial industry are totally unaware of these cycles. Financial professionals are not required to have even a cursory knowledge of economics to give financial advice let alone know what kind of advice to give to clients depending on where we find ourselves in these economic cycles.

I hope other parts of this book help you "connect the dots" and help you see where the economy is headed from here so that your dreams of a comfortable, secure, stress-free retirement may be affected.

Most importantly, this book will provide you with specific strategies you might consider using to protect yourself, as well as prosper, from the coming economic events.

Let's get started.

CHAPTER ONE

The Problems with the Financial Industry

Let me state from the outset that this chapter is largely based on my opinion.

I have worked in the financial industry for over thirty years, so my opinions have not been formed hurriedly, nor have my views been developed based on someone else's experience.

I have worked as a registered representative (stockbroker) and as a supervisor to registered representatives. I have served as the president and CEO of a small broker–dealer. I have served as a consultant to financial professionals, helping them develop marketing and management systems for their businesses. I have also authored seven other books: six for consumers and one for financial professionals. To quote an old cliché, this isn't my first rodeo.

I tell you all this not to brag but to provide you with the necessary background and contextual information for what I'm about to explain to you.

You probably won't hear what I'm going to tell you from many in the financial industry—especially your broker.

It's my view that, given today's precarious economic climate, many brokers and other financial professionals will ultimately fail their clients.

While I believe the majority of the financial industry works hard to try to benefit the client, many of these well-intentioned financial professionals will still miserably fail the client through no fault of their own.

Let me give you just a few reasons.

First, and most importantly, financial professionals are not required to know anything about economics to be licensed. They haven't been properly trained or equipped with the knowledge needed to succeed for their clients in today's environment.

Here's an example.

When I took my Series 7 exam, which is the exam all stockbrokers need to pass to become licensed to sell stocks and bonds, there was only one question about economics. I had to know plenty about sell stops, margin loans, options, and calculating yield to maturity on bonds. But there was only one question on the topic of economics.

I had to know the definition of inflation.

Inflation, as it was defined on the exam, is too much money chasing too few goods and services.

Now I know that this definition is only half correct (more on this later).

In order to provide useful financial advice for their clients, brokers and other financial professionals should be required to become serious students of economics and economic history. They should be required to learn what happened when money printing occurred previously in the United States and in other countries in previous centuries. They should be compelled to study the economic conditions that led to the stock market decline of the 1930s. It should be mandatory for them to study prior bubbles in asset prices in order to help them recognize a bubble and the conditions that lead to its formation.

But none of this knowledge is required in order to become licensed to work in the financial industry.

Consequently, many in the financial industry continue to labor each day doing what they get paid to do: sell securities or make recommendations to clients without regard to the economic conditions that exist at the time. Many financial professionals are oblivious to economic conditions because they've been trained to sell securities rather than learn how different assets perform in different economic environments.

I believe that this can be a big mistake when it comes to the financial well-being of a client. Recent history proves it. Asset bubbles in stocks in 2001 and again beginning in 2007 burst, as bubbles always do, harming many investors who may have taken the advice of their brokers.

I believe that in order to properly advise a client about his or her finances, a solid knowledge base related to economics and fiscal policy is not only desirable but essential.

If a financial professional hasn't studied how different asset classes have behaved in different economic environments historically speaking, how can he or she provide a sound basis for the advice provided to a client?

Through my study of economic history and fiscal policy, I have concluded that there really is nothing new under the sun. Money printing, like we see all around us in the world today, has been tried before, and the outcome has been the same each time.

There are different ways to print money.

During the Roman Empire, the denarius coin, originally composed of pure silver, became a coin containing only worthless alloys over time. That is only one example of many historically when the coinage was debased.

In our fractionalized reserve banking system, money is printed or created when it moves from one bank to another. Banks are only required to reserve 10% of deposits. The rest can be loaned out to customers. The faster money moves from one bank to another, the more money is created.

Let's say you deposit $100,000 into your bank. Your banker is required to reserve $10,000 and can loan out the other $90,000 to a customer who is looking to purchase a starter home. That customer takes the $90,000 from the banker and gives it to the home seller, who deposits it in her bank.

That banker reserves $9,000 and loans out the other $81,000. This process continues. The more borrowing, the more money that is created. That's why central bankers often reduce interest rates: to encourage borrowing in order to create more money.

After the financial crisis of a decade ago, interest rates were reduced to zero. Yet borrowers weren't eager to borrow money. When analyzing private sector debt levels from that point in time, it's easy to see why. Private sector debt levels were so high that the system had reached its capacity to handle debt.

So the Federal Reserve, the central bank of the United States under the direction of then Chair Ben Bernanke, decided to just print money.

There are many examples of money printing throughout history. A study of economic history reveals that money printing occurs on a cyclical basis. Athens in 486 BC, the Roman Empire, France in the early eighteenth century and again later in the eighteenth century, and Colonial America all pursued monetary policies similar to those that have been engaged in recently.

In each of these cases, the reason given for the money printing was similar to the reason given by policymakers today, and in each historical incidence of money printing, the economic outcomes were essentially the same. Yet, if you ask your broker what happened in early-eighteenth-century France, when John Law, the French Central banker, went on a money-printing binge, you'll probably get only a blank stare.

And one doesn't need to go back to eighteenth-century France to see it. In the history of the United States, monetary policies similar to those of today have been pursued three other times. Each time, the economic consequences were the same.

When studying all these historical examples of money printing as a result of debt excesses, it became obvious to me that there are times when it may not be advisable to hold "traditional" asset classes. Sometimes it makes sense to have alternative asset classes in one's portfolio.

Yet this idea of looking at alternative asset classes is foreign to many financial professionals.

Let me give you an example.

While there are always exceptions to any rule, many financial professionals ignore any asset class that is not a stock or bond. Many financial professionals hate the idea of holding cash in a portfolio, saying smugly, "Cash is trash." Many financial professionals also ignore the role that tangible assets can play in a portfolio. Tangible assets, such as real estate and precious metals (not paper versions of each), are often treated like unwanted stepchildren by brokers; they are ignored and rarely thought about.

From my experience, most financial professionals take a "one bucket" approach when helping a client manage his or her nest egg. That's what the financial industry teaches them to do. These professionals have the client invest their assets in a "bucket" that contains stocks and bonds or stock mutual funds and bond mutual funds and may have the client adjust his or her holdings, depending on whether stocks look better, or bonds look better. Unfortunately, these adjustments, when they occur, are made based on the broker's opinion of the potential performance of an asset class rather than on when or how the client may need to use the money.

If the client needs income from his or her investments, the broker may have the client take a systematic withdrawal from the "one bucket" on a pro rata basis. If the client owns 50% stocks and 50% bonds in his or her "one bucket," his or her income withdrawals will be taken 50% from the stock portion of the client's portfolio and 50% from the bond portion of the client's portfolio.

When studying history and economic cycles, there are times when the "one bucket" approach to managing finances can work very well, but there are other times when using the "one bucket" approach to managing money has led to financial disaster. It depends on where we are in the cycle.

I will examine these cycles in this book and offer an asset management approach that can succeed no matter where the economy might be in an economic cycle.

Unfortunately, your existing advisor may not know a thing about these economic cycles because he or she lacks even a fundamental, let alone thorough working knowledge, of economic history.

In addition to lacking a solid working knowledge of economic history, many financial professionals lack a solid understanding of what money is and how the banking system functions.

I know this statement sounds odd initially, but from my experience, it's absolutely true.

I'd venture to guess that if you were to survey a random group of financial professionals and ask them to define "currency," you'd get answers like, currency is an asset, currency is a means of exchange, or currency is something used in commerce.

While currency is used in commerce, as we'll discuss in this book, today's currency is not an asset. Today's currency is debt, which is a fact that goes unnoticed and unrecognized by many Americans and much of the financial industry.

In this book, we'll discuss something that I call the "money-currency cycle." From my studies of different economies and money and currency systems throughout history, I've concluded that money and currency evolve. Money changes over time, and as it changes, it follows the same course or cycle each time. This cycle of change has repeated itself over and over again throughout history.

However, this money-currency cycle change is so gradual that everyday citizens don't notice and neither do many financial professionals. The full money-currency cycle takes, on average, approximately one long human lifetime to complete.

Currency starts out as something tangible. This has often been the case in history. Early settlers in the United States used beaver pelts as currency or a medium of exchange. Mayan Indians used feathers from a specific bird as currency. And, most commonly throughout history, precious metals, such as gold and silver, have been used in commerce.

This is the first step in the money-currency cycle; currency is something tangible. The currency circulating has intrinsic value of its own.

The next evolution of currency is the second step of the money-currency cycle. Currency now becomes paper; however, the paper is redeemable for a tangible item with intrinsic value, which is usually a precious metal. A good example of this step in the money-currency cycle can be found fairly recently in US history. If you're old enough, you may remember something called a silver certificate. Silver certificates were printed in the United States from the 1870s through the 1960s. While these certificates had no inherent value of their own, they could be redeemed for coins containing a fixed amount of silver. So, while the paper silver certificates had no built-in value, the coins for which the silver certificates could be redeemed did have core value.

For every $100 in coins that you owned, you also possessed 72 ounces of silver. For every $100 in silver certificates you possessed, you could redeem the certificates for 72 ounces of silver.

Four hundred quarters equaled $100 face amount, which equaled 72 ounces of silver.

Did you have two hundred half dollars in your sock drawer? You had 72 ounces of silver.

One hundred silver dollars or one thousand dimes gave you the same 72 ounces of silver.

While the paper currency that circulates has no tangible value, the paper note can be exchanged for something with tangible value.

This system under which paper currency can be exchanged for something tangible has its roots in the 1600s when the goldsmith profession became a mainstream business. With gold being used as currency at the time, a goldsmith would offer to store your gold for you in a secure vault for a small fee and give you a receipt for your gold. At any future time, you could bring your receipt to the goldsmith and redeem it for your gold.

As this system developed, it didn't take long for these receipts to be used as money. Rather than going to the goldsmith to redeem your coupon for your gold in order to pay for goods and services, it was far easier to just pay for those goods and services with your receipt since the bearer of the receipt was entitled to turn in the receipt and collect the gold.

This is the second phase of the money-currency cycle.

It is from this second phase of the money-currency cycle that the third phase evolves. As time passes and politicians spend more than they should, which is not a new phenomenon, there is a temptation to print more currency than there are tangible assets to back. Then, eventually, when there is simply too much paper currency in comparison to the tangible asset that backs the paper money, the link between the paper and the tangible asset is eliminated.

Once the link between tangible items and paper currency is eliminated, paper currency is an asset by fiat or by government decree. The paper that circulates is not directly backed by a tangible asset.

This advent of fiat currency is the third step in the money-currency cycle.

Today, every currency in the world is a fiat currency. This has been the case since the link between the Swiss franc and gold was eliminated in 1997. It is also the first time in recorded monetary history that every world currency is a fiat currency.

However, fiat currencies are not a new phenomenon. Even before the use of paper money, fiat currencies existed. During the Roman Empire, the denarius became a fiat currency as the silver content of the coin was reduced and then eventually eliminated.

The final step in the money-currency cycle is the failure of a fiat currency. It has occurred over and over again throughout history; there has never been a fiat currency that has survived long term. We'll discuss this in greater detail in a future chapter.

When a fiat currency fails, the monetary system reverts to some version of the first step in the money-currency cycle. Tangible stuff, such as gold and silver, is once again used as currency. (While, at this point, you may be skeptical about this money-currency cycle concept, keep an open mind. I will give you multiple historical examples in a future chapter to prove to you that this cycle exists.)

Ask most financial professionals to tell you how many different kinds of currency have been used historically, and you'll probably get silence or have your question ignored. Yet, if someone is managing your assets, isn't a thorough understanding of money and currencies one of the most fundamental pieces of knowledge you'd want that person to have?

Without this fundamental understanding of the money-currency cycle and the economic conditions that are created as the money-currency cycle proceeds, I believe many clients are not served well by their advisors or brokers when deciding under what circumstances a particular asset should be held.

Using the "one bucket" approach works well at some points in the cycle but is disastrous during other parts of the money-currency cycle.

Admittedly, the money-currency cycle and related economic cycles are sometimes hard to recognize at first. Sometimes economic cycles exist for several years before it's possible to recognize them for certain.

Due to this, I believe many investors would benefit from using a "two bucket" approach and exit strategies in their investment portfolios rather than the "one bucket" approach advocated by much of the financial industry. An exit strategy is simply a predetermined exit point for an investment, knowing in advance under what circumstances a holding will be purged from a portfolio. (I will discuss the "two bucket" approach in great detail in a subsequent chapter.)

Many financial professionals recommend a particular security, such as a stock or bond, to a client but fail to implement an exit strategy for the recommendation. I believe that's downright reckless and can cause significant losses in an investment portfolio.

It's mind-boggling to me how exit strategies are part of almost any smart plan yet are ignored by much of the financial industry.

Consider these examples.

Smart entrepreneurs start a business and have an exit strategy in place.

The first thing you do when you board a cruise ship is review the exit strategy.

When a school or hospital has a fire drill, the sole focus is on the exit strategy.

On an airplane, the exit strategy is reviewed before the plane leaves the ground.

Yet, when investing, many folks never think about using an exit strategy—simply deciding in advance under what circumstances you will sell that investment.

Think about this for a minute: Doesn't using exit strategies make sense?

There are many easy ways to do this; yet, if you ask the typical broker to help you put exit strategies in place for your portfolio, you may get significant resistance. You may hear things like, "You can't time the market," "You need to focus on the long term," "Keep your eyes on the horizon," or something similar.

However, in my experience, letting someone talk you out of using exit strategies in your investments is like letting the cruise line take the lifeboats off the ship to save space. You might take so many cruises without needing a lifeboat that they eventually seem unnecessary, but sooner or later, a day will come when the lifeboats or the exit strategies are vital.

Let me give you just one example of how you might consider using an exit strategy in an investment.

Take, for instance, an exchange-traded fund or stock that one might own.

Why not put in place a 10% or 15% trailing sell-stop order on that holding? A sell-stop order is an order to sell a security when a certain price is hit. In the case of a 10% trailing sell-stop order, the sell order price on the security is 10% below the current price of the security.

If you bought XYZ stock at $100 per share, you would simultaneously enter a sell-stop order at $90 per share. If XYZ stock moved to $120 per share, your trailing sell-stop order would adjust to 10% below the revised price per share, or $108. If XYZ stock dropped to $115 per share, the sell stop wouldn't move. A 10% trailing sell stop is always 10% below the high-water mark of a security's price.

While no exit strategy is perfect, a sell-stop order is a simple and often effective way to protect an investor from significant losses during a major market downturn.

Admittedly, there are some circumstances in which a sell stop may not limit losses to 10% or 15%, such as during a "flash crash" or a rapidly declining market. In the case of a flash crash, the actual sell price could end up being lower than the targeted exit price.

When using a sell stop, there is also the possibility of the sell target price being hit, the security being sold, and then the price of the security rebounding.

However, in spite of these possible shortfalls, using a sell stop to protect an investment portfolio from a major decline may make sense for many investors.

Given a choice between staying in an investment too long or getting out too soon, which would you prefer?

I'd much rather make the mistake of getting out of an investment position too soon and missing some upside than participating in a major downturn like we all saw in 2001 and from 2007 through 2009. Exiting an investment too soon might mean there are still realized profits; staying in an investment too long often results in certain losses.

As I've stated, if you ask your broker about using a trailing sell stop, you may get some resistance. That's usually when you hear the "You have to invest for the long term" explanation.

That's a typical answer given by a financial professional using the "one bucket" approach.

In my view, the reality is that many brokers get paid to sell products, not manage finances. Again, there are many brokers who do a fine job for their clients, but from my experience, the system often has financial professionals more focused on selling products and generating commissions than on managing money.

To clarify, I should point out that there are two basic models under which many financial professionals and brokers work.

The first is a commission-based model. In this model, the broker is compensated when a product is sold by way of a commission.

The second model under which a financial professional might work is a fee-based model. In this model, the financial professional is compensated through fees. Fees are typically charged based on the amount of time the financial professional spends on a client's matters or on a percentage basis based on the amount of assets the financial professional is managing. In this model, the financial professional is held to a fiduciary standard the client's interests are placed ahead of the interests of the financial professional. When held to a fiduciary standard, any potential conflicts of interest must be disclosed to the client.

In my view, the fee-based model is the model that will serve clients most effectively; but, from my experience, many financial professionals operating under the fee-based model still use the "one bucket" approach even though, in this model, the incentive is more focused on growing assets rather than moving product.

This second fee-based model is also not without its possible drawbacks.

There are many fee-based advisors who charge a fee to help an investor decide which mutual funds to invest in. While this is not inherently bad, there is the potential for the client to overpay on fees since the advisor typically charges a fee in addition to the management fee charged by the mutual fund company.

If a client is paying two layers of fees rather than just one fee, it requires a larger return just to get the client to profitability.

Assume for a moment that the client is investing in mutual funds that have an average internal annual fee of 1%. That means the first 1% a portfolio earns each year will go to the mutual fund money manager(s).

If the client is paying a fee-based advisor an annual fee to help the client select which mutual funds to use, the break-even point is higher. Hypothetically speaking, if the average annual fee in the mutual funds is 1% and the advisor charges an additional 1%, the client's portfolio now has to earn 2% each year before the client reaches break-even status.

While there are many fee-based advisors who earn their management fees and then some, I believe it's important for clients to understand how much they are paying each year in fees and what they are getting in return.

If you are unsure about the level of fees you are paying on your investments, I believe you'd be wise to educate yourself. I advise clients to do something called a "Portfolio Stress Test" to learn exactly what they are paying in management fees on their investments and to discover how their investment holdings performed during prior market declines. I'll tell you how to do your own Portfolio Stress Test in a subsequent chapter.

From my experience, many clients would be wise to undertake this study on their own. As I stated in the introduction, my experience has taught me that no one cares more about your money than you do, so you'd be well served to get educated.

Education is the purpose of this book.

CHAPTER TWO
What Is Money?

As I discussed in the previous chapter, many Americans, as well as many financial professionals, have no idea how money works.

However, in order to understand where we are today, economically speaking, and to understand where we are going and how your nest egg might be affected, it's vital to have a solid understanding of how money and the banking system operate.

The Money-Currency Cycle

Many times throughout history this cycle has repeated...

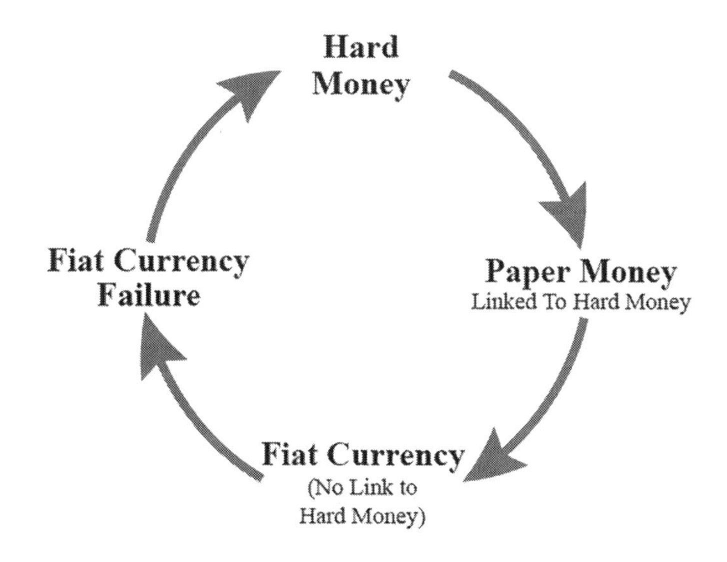

In the first chapter, I discussed the concept of the money-currency cycle. The premise of the money-currency cycle is simple: Over time, money changes.

The illustration on this page shows the progression of the money-currency cycle.

The first step in the money-currency cycle is hard money. During this phase of the money-currency cycle, something tangible, such as gold or silver, is used as currency.

The second step in the money-currency cycle is the introduction of paper currency. In this phase of the money-currency cycle, paper currency can be exchanged for tangible assets, such as gold or silver, at a fixed rate.

The third step in the money-currency cycle is the elimination of the link between paper currency and tangible assets, such as gold or silver, thereby creating a fiat currency.

The fourth step in the money-currency cycle is the failure of the fiat currency, at which point the cycle reverts to its first step, and tangible assets are used as currency once again.

The events and circumstances that lead to the link between paper currency and the elimination of tangible assets, thereby creating a fiat currency, are always the same.

Why?

As we've already stated, because human behavior is predictable. Given similar circumstances, groups of humans tend to behave in the same way. Given similar circumstances, collective groups of politicians have behaved similarly throughout history as well.

Let me prove it to you.

Faced with these three choices to manage an out-of-balance financial situation, which choice do you think politicians in every century have made?

Choice one:	Raise taxes
Choice two:	Cut spending
Choice three:	Print money

You guessed it!

Choice three is always the winner, hands down.

Printing currency is a far easier and more politically acceptable way to solve an out-of-whack financial condition than raising taxes or cutting spending—at least initially.

As I stated in the first chapter, currency printing has been occurring on and off for nearly 2,500 years. A study of history reveals three ways in which currency has been printed. The first currency-printing method has the hard metal currency being debased. This took place during the Roman Empire when the Roman currency, the denarius, was debased. The denarius was initially almost pure silver; however, by the time the Roman Empire fell, the denarius contained no silver and comprised only worthless metal alloys, making the denarius a fiat currency.

The second way in which currency is printed is when the link between the circulating paper currency and the tangible asset is loosened. This happened in the United States in the late 1910s. The Federal Reserve, the central bank of the United States, which was founded in 1913, reduced the backing of the US dollar by gold. The backing of the US dollar by gold was reduced to 40% of its level prior to the Federal Reserve's formation. A little math tells us that, as a result of this reduction in the backing of the US dollar by gold, the currency supply expanded by 250%.

The third and final way in which currency is printed is by the Central Bank after a currency becomes a fiat currency and the link between paper currency and a tangible asset has been eliminated. This is the method that many of the world's central banks, including the Federal Reserve in the United States, use to print currency today.

Whenever currency is printed, easy credit follows. Easy credit leads to the creation of bubbles in asset prices. A textbook example of this bubble building in asset prices as a result of easy credit and loose money took place about a decade ago in the real estate market in the United States. As a result of loose money policies by the Federal Reserve, bankers made downright wild and irresponsible loans. Folks could buy a house with no money down and no credit check; all they needed was a current paycheck stub.

Another wild loan creation by bankers was the reverse amortization loan. Borrowers only had to make a partial interest payment to keep the loan current, resulting in an increasing loan balance as these partial interest rates were made.

As you know, this easy credit created a real estate bubble that saw real estate prices skyrocket. But every easy credit bubble eventually bursts, and the recent real estate bubble was no exception. When debt levels reached the system's capacity to service the debt, the debt accumulation trend abruptly reversed, and prices came crashing down.

Incidentally, since that real estate bubble burst about ten years ago, bankers have repeated the same bad behavior. No-money-down mortgages have re-emerged. Subprime lending in automobiles has reached record levels, and private sector debt is once again at record highs.

We believe we are once again nearing the end of a bubble

cycle with the bursting of the bubble to follow in the relatively near future.

Debt-fueled asset bubbles have built and burst for centuries. The United States has not been immune to these bubbles.

It surprises many people to learn that the United States has a long history of money printing and asset bubbles in spite of the fact that the country attempted to get started on the right foot from a monetary policy perspective.

Back in 1792, the Mint Act was passed, which made gold and silver the currency of the new country. After the Mint Act was passed, any US citizen could have his or her own currency minted from gold and silver by bringing either metal to the mint. A $10 gold piece contained .62 ounces of gold, and the relationship between gold and silver was established at 1 to 15, with an ounce of gold having the same value as 15 ounces of silver.

It was a system of honest currency. Currency was a tangible asset with its own intrinsic value.

At that time, the United States was a young country that was deeply in debt, having fought the Revolutionary War within the previous decade. Treasury Secretary Alexander Hamilton approached President George Washington with what he thought was a great idea to help get rid of the country's debt. Hamilton suggested to Washington that a central bank be set up that could print paper currency. By printing paper currency, Hamilton said, the country could get out of debt more quickly, and the debt-laden economy would also be jump-started.

Thomas Jefferson was vehemently opposed to Hamilton's proposal. Jefferson hated the idea of paper currency and held bankers in low regard. Jefferson almost had Washington convinced that paper currency was a bad idea, when Hamilton, after spending an entire weekend writing an argument in favor of a central bank that could print paper currency, finally convinced President Washington that a central bank would be a good idea.

The nation's first central bank, a 1790s version of today's Federal Reserve, was established.

When setting up the country's first central bank, Hamilton devised a clever scheme to get rid of some of the country's debt. If you wanted to buy shares in this newly established bank, you would have to pay $400 per share. But the kicker was that you had to buy your share with $100 worth of gold or silver and $300 worth of government debt. By forcing share buyers to purchase shares with government debt, Hamilton was able to get share buyers to trade government debt for equity in the bank, effectively erasing some of the government's debt.

However, this scheme was not Hamilton's original idea. As we'll soon see, he borrowed a page from the French economic policy playbook from eighty years prior. There really is nothing new under the sun!

The first central bank in the United States had as assets gold, silver, and government debt. The bank began to print paper currency and make loans to its customers using the newly printed currency. Hamilton did impose a limit on the amount of paper currency that could be printed by the bank; that limit was three times the gold and silver the bank had on deposit.

The paper currency that the bank loaned to customers was redeemable at any time for gold or silver. This created a potential problem for the bank. If everyone who had paper currency wanted to redeem the paper currency for gold and silver at the same time, the bank would be unable to make the redemptions since it had printed three times the paper currency as it had gold or silver to back.

In 1811, when the original twenty-year charter of the first central bank of the United States was up for renewal, it was not renewed.

Then along came the War of 1812. Wars are expensive, and the War of 1812 was no exception. US policymakers were looking at the debt that had been accumulated during the war and realized that they had three choices to deal with the debt:

Choice one:	Raise taxes
Choice two:	Cut spending
Choice three:	Print currency

Which choice do you think they made?

They opted for the third choice. Predictable, isn't it?

The second central bank of the United States was established in 1817. This bank, like its predecessor, could print paper currency. The second central bank of the United States had a twenty-year charter just like the first central bank did. In 1836, then President Andrew Jackson fought hard to ensure that the charter of the second central bank was not renewed. He was successful, and the nation's second central bank was dismantled.

President Jackson was also responsible for putting the country back on a hard money system. The nation went back to the gold exchange standard in 1834. Under this system, an ounce of gold was priced at $20.67. This meant any US citizen could take $20.67 in currency into a bank and redeem it for an ounce of gold or take an ounce of gold into a bank and redeem it for $20.67 in currency.

Gold remained at that price for ninety-nine years until 1933, when then President Franklin D. Roosevelt took the nation off the gold standard in order to print paper currency to attempt to alleviate the harsh economic symptoms of the Depression, which was part of the predictable economic cycle we will discuss in the next chapter.

Between 1834 and 1933, the country did go off the gold exchange standard once. President Abraham Lincoln took the country off the gold standard in order to fund the Civil War.

There is an important lesson here: It's impossible to spend massively when you have a gold exchange standard.

You might agree that it would be nice to have a monetary system in place that would force politicians to limit spending. In nearly every country in nearly every century, there has been some group of politicians who have proven they are incapable of fiscal responsibility. The gold exchange standard imposes the fiscal responsibility necessary for long-term economic health. By limiting the money printing to the gold that backs it, spending restraint by the elected is automatic.

During the Civil War, President Lincoln took a look at the amount of gold in the vault and quickly concluded that he could never finance the war. He was going to need a lot more money than he had the gold to back. As a result, he took the nation off the gold standard, which allowed him to print paper currency, known as "greenbacks" at the time. This allowed Lincoln to fund the Civil War. At this time in American history, both gold and paper currency were used in everyday commerce.

In 1879, the United States went back on the gold standard after paper currency excesses created economic havoc and asset bubbles. There will be more on this later.

The third central bank of the United States, today's Federal Reserve, was formed in 1913. J.P. Morgan and John Rockefeller, two men who had become exceptionally wealthy during the Long Depression of 1873, lobbied the government for a central bank.

A central bank that could print paper currency would be good for business, as far as Morgan and Rockefeller were concerned, since inflation could be created to allow for easy business expansion. As we've already discussed, one of the first things the central bank did was reduce the backing of the US dollar by gold. The US dollar's gold backing was reduced to 40%, greatly expanding the currency supply and leading to the prosperity illusion of the Roaring Twenties.

I use the term "prosperity illusion" intentionally. As we've established, easy money leads to easy credit, which leads to asset bubbles. Asset bubbles burst when the system reaches its capacity to add debt. When debt capacity is reached, the debt has to be purged from the financial system. In the case of the debt excesses of the Roaring Twenties, the debt purging came in the 1930s, which was the period of time known as the Great Depression.

A central bank printing paper currency does lead to economic expansion; however, **in this system, *economic expansion always stops* because the economy expands through debt accumulation.**

After World War II, the United States went back on a quasi-gold exchange standard system. As part of the Bretton Woods Agreement, the US dollar was made the world's reserve currency, a status it still enjoys today; however, this status is quickly slipping. As the world's reserve currency after the Bretton Woods Agreement, the US dollar was exchangeable for gold at a fixed rate of $35 per ounce.

However, US citizens could not legally own gold bullion. President Franklin Roosevelt had made it illegal to own gold in 1933 to allow him to print paper currency to spend massively on government programs designed to combat the Depression. After the Bretton Woods Agreement, only foreign investors could redeem US dollars for gold.

During the 1960s, the Vietnam War was raging, and Medicare and Medicaid became the law of the land. The war and these new programs were expensive. Policymakers had three choices to pay the bill:

Choice one:	Raise taxes
Choice two:	Cut spending
Choice three:	Print money

By now, you know what totally predictable choice was made—the same choice that politicians have always made throughout history.

The currency printing began, and it did not go unnoticed by foreign investors, who were able to exchange their US dollars for gold. Many of these investors decided they would be much more comfortable holding the gold than their US dollars. A run on the bank ensued, with these foreign investors rushing to turn in their US dollars and demanding gold.

In 1971, then President Richard Nixon saw the writing on the wall. There was simply not enough gold in the vault to back the paper US dollars circulating. In order to "preserve the integrity of the US dollar," President Nixon temporarily suspended the redemption of US dollars for gold. The redemption has never resumed.

Since 1971, the US dollar has been a fiat currency, as are all currencies in the world at present.

The chart on this page illustrates how the purchasing power of the US dollar has been affected.

Notice that point to point, from 1792 through 1933, there was zero price inflation. A US dollar bought about the same level of goods and services in 1933 as in 1792.

Surprised?

Notice that during the Civil War, when President Lincoln took the nation off the gold standard, the US dollar lost about 50% of its purchasing power.

Sadly, since 1933, when President Roosevelt made it illegal for American citizens to own gold, the US dollar has lost more than 90% of its purchasing power.

The Greenback's Purchasing Power

This log scale chart of the purchasing power of the dollar begins with an index value of 100 at the passage of the Mint Act of 1792. The solid lines present periods when the dollar was convertible into a specific quantity of gold, and the fluctuations represent changes in the purchasing power of gold. The dotted lines present periods when the dollar was not pegged to gold, during and after the War of 1812, the Civil War, World War I and World War II. There was limited convertibility from 1945 to 1971, but the dollar lost purchasing power during the period. The last link between the U.S. currency and gold was cut in 1971 and the loss of purchasing power accelerated. By 2004, the dollar had lost more than 92% of its original purchasing power.

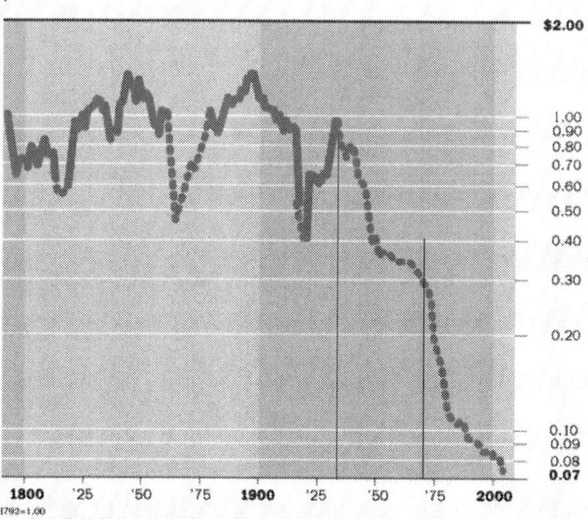

Source: Chart by American Institute for Economic Research, from the Wholesale Price Index compiled by the Bureau of Labor Statistics

No discussion of money, currency, and monetary policy would be complete without a discussion of inflation and deflation. Many don't completely understand these terms. If I were to ask the average person to define "inflation," I would most often get the answer: too much money chasing too few goods and services.

Unfortunately, that's also how many financial professionals would define inflation.

But it's a poor definition.

Properly defined, inflation and deflation describe the level of currency in circulation.

Inflation is defined as an expansion of the currency supply. As we'll discuss, our banking system is biased toward currency creation and expansion.

Deflation is inflation's polar opposite: a contraction of the currency supply. Deflation is currency's disappearing act.

While many believe that today's massive currency printing by the Federal Reserve will lead to inflation and higher prices, which are symptoms of inflation, as we'll soon discuss, history tells us that today's economic conditions are far more likely to lead to deflation.

Despite the Federal Reserve's past money-printing binge of $85 billion per month via quantitative easing, now reduced to zero as of this writing although low interest rates are still leading to some money creation, history suggests that a massive contraction of the money supply is likely.

The explanation for this is quite simple. Let's start with the fact that **most of today's money is debt, not actual currency**. The idea that today's money is debt is a foreign concept to many, including many financial professionals.

Let me give you an example.

Say you have $50,000 cash in a bank account. You could go to your bank, withdraw $50,000 in cash, bring the cash home, and stuff it under your mattress.

That would give you $50,000 in actual currency under your mattress.

Now, let's say a relative of yours comes to you and asks to borrow $50,000. While you're open to helping out the relative, you'd like some collateral in order to protect yourself.

Your relative offers to give you the title to her car and will allow you to place your name on the title as a lienholder. With this offer of collateral, you decide to take the $50,000 from under your mattress and loan the money to your relative at an interest rate of 5%. Since the money was earning 0% interest under the mattress, you're happy with the 5% return, plus you have some collateral to help protect yourself.

As long as your relative is creditworthy, you still have a $50,000 asset. The asset is just no longer cash; it's debt that's owed to you. But it is still an asset.

If you were to put together a personal balance statement, you'd list the $50,000 loan payable to you as an asset. If you hadn't made the loan to your relative and still had the cash under the mattress, you'd list the cash as an asset of the same value on your personal balance statement.

Whether the $50,000 is actual currency or a $50,000 loan that you've made, it's still a $50,000 asset. When you give your paper currency asset to your relative, you are converting a cash asset to a debt asset.

Here is the first very important point: Cash and debt are both money. Debt, or credit extended, spends exactly the same way as actual currency.

That brings me back to my point: Most money today is debt. Debt owed by one person or entity to another person or entity is an asset to the person or entity to whom the debt is owed. In our financial system, most money is the liability of another person or entity.

This money remains an asset as long as the borrower is creditworthy. However, should the borrower not pay up, the asset's value may be reduced, and money disappears from the system.

Technically defined, this is deflation: money disappearing from the financial system.

Let's say your relative comes to you after you've given her the loan of $50,000 and tells you that she can no longer make payments on the loan. She has lost her job, and in spite of her best efforts, there is no way she will be able to pay you back. She voluntarily brings you the car you took as collateral on the loan, so you can sell it to attempt to recover your asset.

After a few weeks, you realize that the car might bring $20,000, which is nowhere close to the $50,000 you are owed on the loan. You decide to cut your losses and sell the car. You pocket the $20,000 and write off the $30,000 loss to bad judgment.

That is $30,000 that has just disappeared from your personal balance sheet, and that $30,000 has just disappeared from the financial system.

When most money is debt and debt levels are too high to possibly be paid, money will disappear from the financial system, and the money supply will contract. This is deflation.

Because banks have debt as assets, when debt gets too high to be paid, banks lose assets and become insolvent. As we'll discuss in the next chapter, this debt accumulation and subsequent bust in banks, stocks, and real estate is predictable and cyclical.

The Federal Reserve and many of the other central banks around the world are attempting to add money to the system faster than money disappears through the system through defaults on debt.

Unfortunately, they are fighting an uphill battle.

Given the level of debt that exists today worldwide, simple math tells you there is more debt than can ever possibly be paid, this is a simple, eternally true economic rule that cannot be changed.

This is exactly where we are today. There is far more debt than can ever possibly be paid. Since most money is debt, this means money will have to disappear from the system as de-

US Private Sector Debt

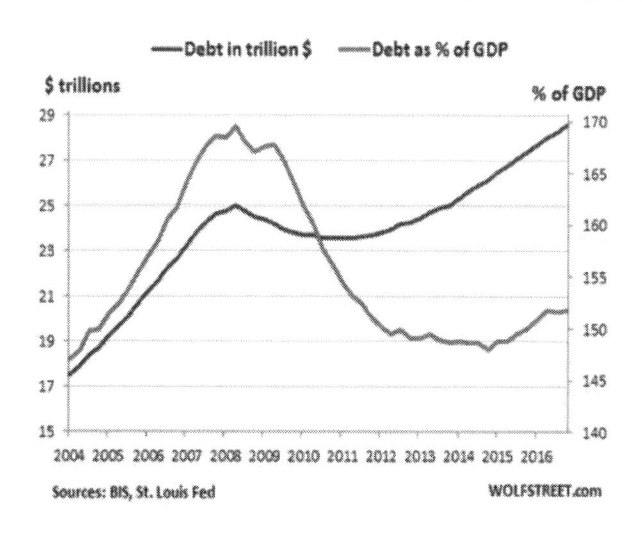

faults occur on the debt. Money will do a disappearing act, banks will suffer, and deflation will be the result.

Just to make the point, consider the chart on this page. The red line on the chart represents private sector debt measured as a percentage of gross domestic product (GDP), the most common metric used to measure the size of the US economy. The blue line represents actual debt in terms of US dollars.

Notice that although debt as a percentage of the economy as measured by GDP is lower than at the time of the financial crisis, debt in terms of dollars has risen.

Remember our basic economic rule?

If there is too much debt to be paid, not all the debt will be paid.

Not all the debt was paid during the Great Depression, resulting in a deflationary climate. Today, with debt levels that are higher, the outcome cannot be much different.

The facts don't lie.

It remains to be seen what the Federal Reserve's response will be should deflation kick in. If the Fed elects to print currency in earnest again, they risk a confidence loss in the US dollar currency.

As we'll see in a future chapter, money printing to the point of the destruction of the currency has also occurred many times historically. Massive inflation is the outcome, and then when a new currency is established, and the debt is recalibrated, deflation kicks in.

When debt levels are excessive, deflation is the inevitable outcome; it cannot be avoided. When one studies history, time and time again, politicians and policymakers have printed money in response to excessive debt levels, and each time the outcome has been the same: inflation first, then deflation.

Here is another key point: Money printing doesn't do anything to address debt levels; it only temporarily masks the symptoms of excessive debt. Once the system reaches its capacity to handle debt, economic contraction has to occur, and deflation has to set in.

Think about this for a moment.

If you can't afford another monthly payment, does it really matter what the interest rate is on the loan?

The amount of debt the system can handle is limited for one simple reason: Debt consumes future production.

Consider this example to make the point.

You are in the market for a new automobile. You go to your favorite car dealership and buy a car for $30,000. You pay cash for the car and drive it off the lot.

A neighbor of yours notices your new car in your driveway and stops by to take a look. She loves the car so much that she decides to go to the same car dealership and buy the same exact car in a different color. She elects to finance the car since she doesn't have the necessary level of cash to pay for the car outright.

You and your neighbor each own identical brand-new cars. You, by paying cash for the car, spent prior production for your purchase. In order to have cash available to make your purchase, you had to go to work in the past, earn money, and save enough of it to allow you to buy the car. You are spending yesterday's production to pay for today's purchase.

Your neighbor, by financing the car, is spending future production. Because she has a new payment book in her possession, she needs to get up tomorrow and go to work to earn enough money to make the payments on the car. She is spending tomorrow's production to pay for today's purchase.

When enough of tomorrow's production is consumed today, the system's capacity to handle debt is reached and debt accumulation ceases. The trend then reverses, and debt is purged from the system.

That's where we are today.

Over the last ten years, since the financial crisis, the easy money policies of the Federal Reserve have simply masked the symptoms of debt excesses and have done so at the expense of the purchasing power of the US dollar.

Depending on the future policy response of the Federal Reserve, the central bank of the United States, we may have to face further currency devaluation before we face the consequences of debt.

Eventually, inevitably, we will see deflation. Current debt levels will make it impossible to avoid that outcome. The chart on this page illustrates global debt levels approximately over the last twenty years. Notice how much higher debt levels are today as compared to debt levels at the time of the financial crisis.

A similar outcome to the financial crisis of a decade ago is a near certainty.

The chart provides evidence that the policy response of the Federal Reserve simply papered over the debt problems with newly printed currency masking the symptoms of debt and delaying its inescapable consequences.

However, this papering over of the debt problem, although it has created a period of apparent prosperity, has not been without cost. The US dollar has lost a good deal of purchasing power as well as integrity around the world.

This loss in purchasing power of the US dollar can't be seen in the official US inflation rate.

That's because the official inflation rate calculation has been manipulated over the years and now excludes an allowance for food prices and fuel prices. The official inflation rate is measured by the Consumer Price Index. From 2013 through 2017, the official inflation rate was:

2013	1.5%
2014	1.6%
2015	0.1%
2016	1.3%
2017	2.5%

If you've been to the grocery store over the past five years, you're probably thinking that these numbers don't look too accurate.

A more realistic measure of the inflation rate might be found by using a private inflation index. The Chapwood Index is such a metric.

The Chapwood Index measures inflation by comparing the price of five hundred consumer items one year ago with the price of those same five hundred consumer items today. The difference in price from one year to the next is then used to determine the inflation rate.

Global Debt Still Piling Up

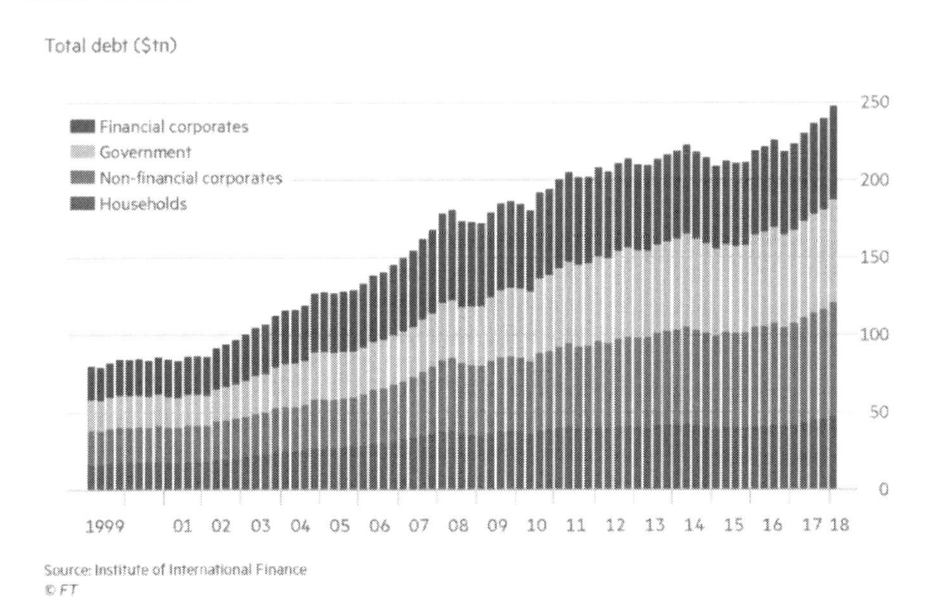

Depending on the part of the country in which you live, the Chapwood Index measure of inflation has been about 10% per year, a far cry from the official rate. Yet, if you look at the price of groceries, doctor's office calls, and automobiles, to name a few, you're probably inclined to agree with the Chapwood Index's measure of inflation, or at least agree that it's closer to reality than the official inflation rate.

Inflation is just a sanitized way of saying currency devaluation. When money is printed, the purchasing power of the currency declines. That has happened to the US dollar, and due to this devaluation, there has been significant movement away from the US dollar worldwide.

Think about this for a minute.

Don't you want to store your wealth in a vehicle that at least maintains purchasing power? Ideally, the vehicle in which you store your wealth would allow you to increase your purchasing power, but at the very least, you want to maintain it.

After World War II, the US dollar was the world's reserve currency. A reserve currency is the currency that countries inventory or reserve to use in trade. As part of a worldwide agreement, the US dollar was redeemable for gold at a rate of $35 per ounce.

Because the US dollar could be exchanged for gold, and was therefore stable, the rest of the world was very comfortable using it in international trade. The vast majority of international transactions took place with the US dollar.

Then the 1960s came along. Medicare and Medicaid became law and required significant funding. The Vietnam War was being fought at a hefty cost as well. US politicians had three choices to get the funding they needed: They could raise taxes, cut spending, or print currency.

As you probably guessed, they decided to print currency.

This printing of currency made many foreign governments and other holders of US dollars understandably nervous, and they began to exchange their US dollars for gold, as they were entitled to do.

Trouble was, the United States had printed more dollars than the country had gold to back, so in 1971, then President Richard Nixon went on television and announced that redemption of US dollars for gold was being temporarily suspended. As we all now know, that temporary suspension turned out to be permanent.

Since the US dollar was no longer backed by gold, the United States had to figure out a way to keep demand for the US dollar high. So the United States negotiated a deal with Saudi

Arabia to have the country price its oil in US dollars in exchange for military protection and other favors. That deal meant that any country that desired to buy oil from Saudi Arabia would have to inventory US dollars in order to do so.

The plan worked. The US dollar—despite being a fiat currency, meaning it had no backing by anything tangible but was legal tender by government decree—remained the world reserve currency.

However, over the last several years there has been a dramatic shift away from the US dollar all around the world while the Chinese currency, officially the renminbi, has been gaining some attention. This is a real and growing trend and one that anyone who is aspiring to retire should understand. Here are just a few of the many shifts away from the US dollar and moves toward the renminbi:
-In 2018, the first oil futures contract priced in Chinese renminbi was sold.

-In 2016, China launched its own gold exchange, allowing gold buyers to use the Chinese currency to purchase gold.

-In 2018, the country of Pakistan elected to begin using the Chinese currency rather than the US dollar in bilateral trade with China.

-The Chinese currency is now part of the International Monetary Fund's basket of reserve currencies. The Chinese renminbi joins the US dollar, the euro, the British pound, and the Japanese yen in this reserve currency basket.

-Nigeria, the largest non-Arab, OPEC oil-producing nation signed a new deal with China to increase their domestic and international transactions using renminbi rather than the US dollar, which had been used previously.

-Russia is now the top crude oil exporter to China. At the start of the decade, Saudi Arabia enjoyed a 20% share of Chinese crude imports, while Russia was lagging far behind with 7%. Now the Saudis find themselves neck and neck with Moscow for the lead in Chinese market share, with both performing in the 13–16% range. But Russia's share continues to rise, as Russia accepts the Chinese currency as payment for oil while Saudi Arabia still uses only the US dollar.

The Federal Reserve's printing of money has had the rest of the world look for US dollar alternatives. Should printing begin again in earnest, this move away from the US dollar will likely intensify.

Without massive money printing, we will have to move to deflation given the significant levels of private sector debt.

So our economic future is certain: We will have inflation followed by deflation, or we will go straight to deflation.

CHAPTER THREE

Predictable Economic Seasons

As we've discussed, I believe the money-currency cycle is predictable because human nature is predictable.

Faced with the same set of facts and circumstances, humans tend to make the same choices time after time.

There is an economic theory that has been developed based on predictable human behavior. Understanding this theory is vital to understanding where we are today economically. It is commonly known as the Kondratieff (pronounced con-dra'-tee-eff) Wave Theory.

I believe the evidence that this theory is valid is overwhelming. I'll present much of that evidence to you in this chapter.

The decade was the 1920s.

A Russian economist by the name of Nikolai Kondratieff was appointed by Russian ruler Joseph Stalin to study capitalism. As an opponent of capitalism, Stalin wanted Kondratieff to conclude that capitalism was simply a misguided experiment that could not succeed long term. Unfortunately for Kondratieff, he did not come to this conclusion. Instead, in his landmark work, published in 1925, titled *The Major Economic Cycles,* Kondratieff concluded that capitalist economies move in boom and bust cycles that are predictable.

Stalin didn't like the results of Kondratieff's work, so Kondratieff was relegated to an existence in prison before facing the firing squad in 1938. Kondratieff's work was not widely accepted at the time; however, his important work has lived on and has been built upon by many modern-day economists.

Many economists who have studied the work of Kondratieff have concluded, as Kondratieff did, that capitalist economies move in boom and bust cycles and that each of these predictable economic cycles can be broken down into four subcycles. As we will discuss in this chapter, each of these four subcycles has existed four times in American history.

These subcycles can take anywhere from fifteen to twenty-five years to complete, so in order to complete one full cycle of four subcycles, anywhere from sixty to eighty years can elapse, which is the approximate length of one human life. When the full cycle of four subcycles is complete, the cycle begins again.

For the purposes of this discussion, we'll label these subcycles of each economic cycle spring, summer, autumn, and winter. Kondratieff and many modern-day economists have tracked these economic seasons, or subcycles, which have their root in predictable human behavior, all the way back to the beginning of the Industrial Revolution in the mid- to late 1700s. As you'll discover when you read this chapter, these economic subcycles are very closely correlated to the money cycle since both cycles have their root in predictable human behavior.

Here is a brief description of each season and the characteristics of each one.[2]

The Spring Cycle

During spring, an economy experiences a gradual increase in business and employment. Consumer confidence gradually increases. Consumer prices begin a gradual increase compared to the levels seen during the previous cycle (the winter cycle). Stock prices rise and reach a peak at the end of the spring cycle, and credit gradually expands. At the beginning of the spring cycle, overall debt levels are low.

The Summer Cycle

During summer, an economy sees an increase in the currency supply, which leads to inflation. Gold prices reach a significant peak at the end of the summer period. Interest rates rise rapidly and peak at the end of the summer season. Stocks are under pressure and decline throughout the period, reaching a low at the end of the summer cycle.

The Autumn Cycle

During autumn, money is plentiful and gold prices fall, reaching a gold bear market low by the end of the autumn season. During autumn, there is a massive stock bull market and much speculation. Financial fraud is prevalent, and real estate prices rise significantly due to speculation. Debt levels are astronomical. Consumer confidence is at an all-time high due to high stock prices, high real estate prices, and plentiful jobs.

The Winter Cycle

During winter, an economy experiences a crippling credit crisis, and money becomes scarce. Financial institutions are in trouble. There are unprecedented bankruptcies at the personal, corporate, and government levels. There is a credit crunch, and interest rates rise. There is an international monetary crisis. There are pension funding problems, and the price of gold and gold-related equities rise.

Based on these descriptions, in which season would you say we currently find ourselves?

If you said winter, I agree.

Here is my view:

- The most recent spring cycle occurred from 1949 to 1966.
- The most recent summer cycle occurred from 1967 to 1982.
- The most recent autumn cycle occurred from 1983 to 2000.
- The most recent winter cycle, in which we currently find ourselves, began in 2001.

During an economic autumn season, debt accumulates until the system reaches its capacity for debt; then, once no more debt can be added to the system, the economic season changes from autumn to winter. During the economic winter season, debt must be purged from the system, which is a painful process, as we'll soon see.

Take a look at the following chart.

The top line illustrates the total level of debt that exists in the United States. It includes debt at all levels of government as well as business and household debt. The bottom line illustrates total national income. Look how much faster debt has grown than income.

Consider this: If the top line on the chart represented your household debt and the bottom line represented your household income, at what point would your debt become unsustainable?

This chart illustrates why I believe we are in an economic winter season, during which debt will have to be purged from the system.

Total American Debt vs National Income

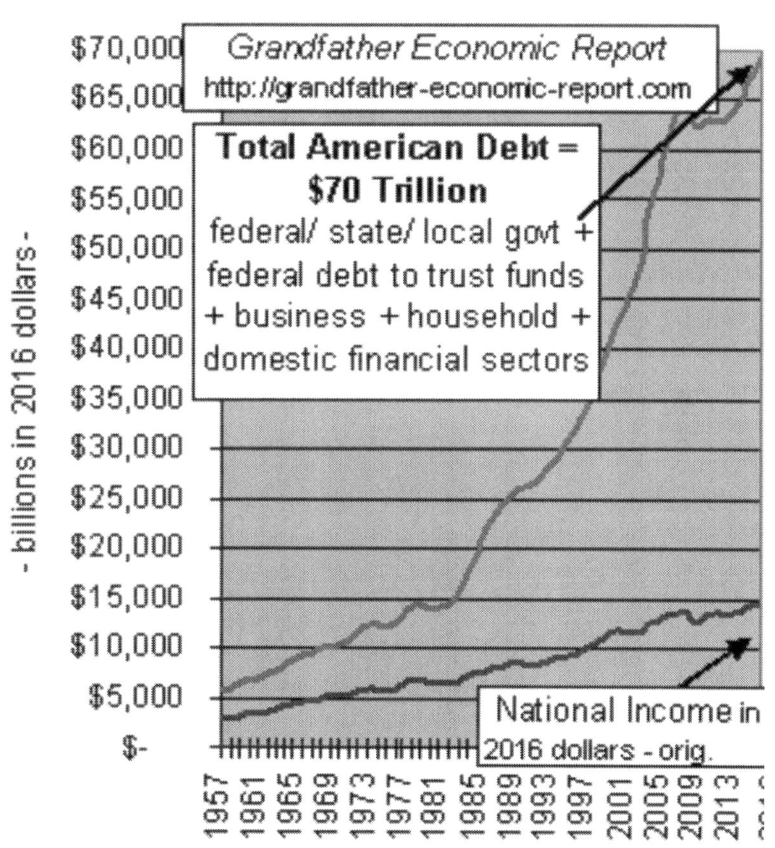

Notice that since the financial crisis of about one decade ago that debt has expanded. Much of the economic growth that we've experienced hasn't been growth at all but rather debt-fueled consumption.

The money-printing reponse of the Federal Reserve at the time of the financial crisis has simply allowed even more debt to accumulate. Without this money printing literally out of thin air, the deflationary cycle would already be upon us.

This massive accumulation of debt last occurred worldwide during the autumn season of the 1920s. Once the debt in the system reached its capacity, the trend of debt accumulation reversed and led to the economic winter season of the 1930s, which we all know as the Great Depression.

Given that debt levels are even higher today, a similar outcome of banking failures and a collapse in asset prices is unavoidable in my view.

It surprises many of my clients to learn that this autumn season debt accumulation cycle, followed by a winter cycle during which debt is purged from the system, has occurred three other times in US history. There are multiple other historical examples proving the existence of this cycle, going all the way back to Greece in 486 BC.

Because this cycle of debt accumulation followed by deflationary debt purging repeats, the conditions that exist in today's economy are nothing new, nor should the ultimate outcome be surprising to anyone with knowledge of money and economic history.

Yet, in spite of these facts, many financial professionals who are unaware of this reality continue to use the "one bucket" approach to managing clients' assets.

The reality is that today's economic winter season had to occur because debt levels in the prior autumn season reached the system's capacity to handle debt. This is a predictable pattern that repeats itself over and over. One look at US history proves it.

The first economic autumn cycle in US history occurred from 1821 to 1836. This autumn cycle was predictably followed by a winter cycle.

As you may recall from our prior discussion, the second central bank of the United States was chartered in 1817 when the country was dealing with massive debts accumulated during the War of 1812. The second central bank, like today's central bank, the Federal Reserve, printed currency. Then, after the bank's charter was not renewed, state and regional banks were allowed to issue currency. This resulted in even more easy money and more widely available credit.

As we've discussed, without widely available easy credit, the system cannot reach its capacity for debt, and asset price bubbles cannot form.

In the economic autumn season of the 1830s, as a result of this easy credit, a real estate bubble formed and subsequently burst. Speculators abounded. It was a typical autumn season asset bubble fueled by easy credit.

This article excerpt[1] explains (emphasis added):

In 1837, however, the young nation endured its most serious depression yet.

This panic was made worse by a number of factors: large debts incurred by states due to over-expansion of canals and the construction of railroads; an unfavorable balance of trade as imports exceeded exports, resulting in a loss of specie (gold and silver—as opposed to paper currency); and several crop failures in 1835 and 1837. The major cause of the panic, however, was the economic impact of land speculation. It was a period of speculative mania.

After the demise of the Bank of the United States, state and wildcat banks grew rapidly during the 1830s. Funds were more easily available, and investors borrowed money at an incredible pace. Not only the small Western farmer, but merchants, manufacturers and traders also borrowed heavily. ***The business community, rather than paying off their debts and refinancing new ventures, anticipated greater returns if they invested their borrowed money in speculative enterprises—investments that, they hoped, would greatly increase in value while they held them. Leading the list of speculative ventures were investments in the vast amounts of readily available cheap land.***

Land offices throughout the country reported record sales as speculators invested for quick returns. Between 1834 and 1836, sales totaled 37 million acres. ***By 1836, sales were ten times greater than they were in 1830****. "Land office business" was the order of the day. In an effort to curb this speculative fever, President Jackson issued the Specie Circular. This order mandated all land offices to accept only gold and silver, rather than "rag" money, in payment for public lands. Since state banks did not have adequate specie backing, land sales dropped. Numerous speculators defaulted on their payments, because little gold and silver were available.*

The speculative mania continued to spread, despite the Federal Government's attempts to halt it*, or at least to curb the speculative holding of large tracts of land. Speculators, armed with ample cash, hired shrewd agents to keep them apprised of the best lands—and land bargains—available. Large* *speculators also used a slew of unethical and illegal methods to gain the upper hand in their quest for land.*

Public land, although the most important facet of speculation, was by no means the only kind of land sold. Urban real estate was also caught up in this mania as values increased. A Hartford speculator related making 75% annually on an investment of $1,000 in Michigan, where the boom was in high gear. Not only the Midwest witnessed wild speculation. Valuation of real property increased in New York over 50% in five years. And even Maine timber lands tripled in price in just a few years.

Asset price bubbles are common in an economic autumn season. The economic autumn season from 1821 to 1836 was followed by the winter season of 1837 to 1845, during which debt was purged from the system.

When debt-fueled asset bubbles burst, banks which have debt as assets, go bust. During the economic winter season beginning in 1837, out of the 850 banks in existence in the United States at the time, 350 banks failed completely and another 62 experienced a partial failure.[2]

This brings us back to the eternal economic truth: If there is too much debt to be paid, it will not be paid. That's why economic winter seasons exist.

The next autumn season began in 1866. Price bubbles in assets formed, and easy credit was again the cause. In 1863 and 1864, National Banking Acts were passed into law. Until these acts were passed, only state banks existed, with the federal government having no control over them. The National Banking Acts created nationally chartered banks. These nationally chartered banks had gold, silver, and government debt as assets, similar to the asset composition of the first central bank of the United States that we previously discussed. Each national bank could issue its own currency but was limited in the amount of currency it could print. Each national bank could only print currency to the extent it owned government debt to back the currency.

It was this change in the backing of currency that allowed the country to finance the Civil War. By changing the currency rules from requiring gold to back the paper currency to allowing government debt to back the paper currency, more currency could be printed. The currency supply expanded.

After the war, easy credit was readily available as a result of currency printing. Like other times when there was abundant easy credit, asset price bubbles formed. The following summary explains[3] (emphasis added):

The era of high prices and business activity which had followed the war yielded its legitimate effect in an abnormal growth of the spirit of speculation. The inevitable consequence followed. In 1873 came a financial crash that carried ruin far and wide throughout the country. ***It began on October 1, in the disastrous failure of the banking firm of Jay Cooke & Co., of Philadelphia, the financiers of the Northern Pacific Railroad. Failure after failure succeeded, panic spread through the whole community, and the country was thrown into a condition resembling that of 1837, but more disastrous from the fact that much greater wealth was affected.*** *Years passed before business regained its normal proportions.* ***A process of contraction set in****, and it was not till 1878 that the timidity of capital was fully overcome, and business once more began to thrive.*

Industry and trade had flourished beyond precedent during the first years after the war. The high protective tariff contributed its share to the general rush of enterprise. In 1873 railroad mileage had doubled itself since 1860, and this was a prolific cause of rash speculation. While business was expanding the currency was contracting. Paper money had depreciated, and the conditions foreboded a crash. The Jay Cooke firm stood at the head of the great banking concerns. This house had handled most of the government loans during the war, and as already stated, were financing the doubtful Northern Pacific scheme. When this firm broke, strong institutions tottered and thousands of people in every rank of life were stricken with absolute ruin or sufferings that were none the less poignant for being outside the category of direct financial failures. The blow was felt for years in impaired credit, pressure for payment of dues, the lowering of securities and general dread of even safe enterprises. United States bonds fell from five to ten per cent. ***Savings were exhausted, and many banks went under. Labor felt the cruel stroke for long after in the shutting down of factories and the half-time employment.*** *The country was in a state of alarm and disgust at the bitter consequences of questionable acts in Congress, by the Administration, and in the realm of finance, and its indignant resolve to change things for the better was expressed in the heated contest which replaced the Grant administration with that of President Hayes, in 1876.*

During the autumn season of 1866, mortgages were easy to get. Large banks were more than glad to make loans to developers. Half-built buildings were accepted as collateral for many of these mortgages because almost anyone could get credit. A housing bubble formed.

But there was another bubble as well. Railroad construction had been financed mainly by large banks like the Jay Cooke firm mentioned previously. Complicated bonds that many investors didn't understand were used to finance the railroad construction. Eventually, this rapid construction became unsustainable. Railroad companies and large banks failed. The stock market crashed, and a deflationary period followed. During the economic winter season starting in 1873, banks and railroads failed.[4] With just a few variations, it was 1837 all over again.

The predictable pattern is clear.

Easy money precedes easy credit, which precedes asset price bubbles, which precedes a financial crisis. The financial crisis occurs when debt levels reach the system's capacity to handle the debt. Deflation follows as debt is purged from the system.

This pattern repeated itself yet again in the 1920s. As we've discussed, the newly formed Federal Reserve, the nation's third central bank, was founded in 1913. After the central bank was founded, the backing of the US dollar by gold was reduced to 40% of its prior level, allowing for an expansion of the currency supply.

This massive expansion of the currency supply led to private sector debt expanding to unsustainable levels during the economic autumn season of the 1920s before reaching the system's debt capacity. The debt accumulation trend then reversed and transformed itself into the debt-purging, deflationary period of the 1930s, the last economic winter season, which we all refer to as the Great Depression.

Like the two autumn seasons before, the economic autumn season of the 1920s saw prosperity seemingly everywhere. But as most of the planet was feeling happy and prosperous, debt was slowly increasing to dangerous, unsustainable levels.

Bubbles in the real estate market and the stock market formed before ultimately bursting. The Harvard Business School described the bubbles of the 1920s like this at the time of the recent subprime mortgage collapse[5] (emphasis added):

The famous stock market bubble of 1925–1929 has been closely analyzed. ***Less well known, and far less well documented, is the nationwide real estate bubble that began around 1921 and deflated around 1926****. In the midst of our current subprime mortgage collapse, economists and historians interested in the role of real estate markets in past financial crises are reexamining the relationship of the first asset-price bubble of the 1920s with the later stock market bubble and the Great Depression that followed. Limited data on 1920s home prices and foreclosures means that many questions remain unanswered. Historical trade publications like the weekly New York Real Estate Record and Builder's Guide, of which Baker Library holds a sixty-year run, allow researchers to fill in the blanks. The implications of early findings may challenge conventional wisdom about the factors that caused and prolonged the Great Depression.*

In the 1920s, Florida was the site of a real estate bubble fueled by easy credit *and advertisers promoting a lifestyle of sunshine and leisure.* ***Contemporary accounts describe a collective madness that consumed Florida investors; city lots in Miami were bought and sold as many as 10 times in a single day.****_The received wisdom holds that a 1926 hurricane pricked the bubble, but house price indices and construction data suggests that the boom and bust was in fact a nationwide phenomenon whose causes and consequences remain unclear.*

The housing price downturn in 1926 led to a rise in the foreclosure rate. Foreclosures were the cause of considerable hardship in the 1920s, but public attention focused on the plight of family farms, not residential real estate. ***Heavily mortgaged during World War I, in expectation of continued high prices, many family farms were overwhelmed by the postwar collapse of the agricultural commodities market. Yet foreclo-***

sures of residential properties also increased in 1926, rising steadily through the stock market bubble and peaking in 1933.

Once again, the pattern is clear. The prosperity of the economic autumn season, driven by increasing debt levels fueled by easy credit, gives way to an economic winter season characterized by high unemployment, bank failures, and asset price bubbles bursting.

Shortly after World War II, the nation emerged from the economic winter season and moved into the economic spring season. During spring, as we've already discussed, an economy experiences a gradual increase in business and employment. Consumer confidence gradually increases. Consumer prices begin a gradual increase compared to levels seen during the winter cycle. Stock prices rise and reach a peak at the end of the spring cycle. Credit gradually expands. At the beginning of the spring cycle, overall debt levels are low.

Here are some headlines from the most recent economic spring season in the United States, which occurred, in our view, from 1949 through 1966.

> "The Economy Is in a Transition Period Following the War-Born Inflation"
> –*The Pittsburgh Post-Gazette*, July 12, 1949

> "Economy Strong Says Ike but Warns of Complacency"
> –*The Chicago Tribune*, January 29, 1954

"Stock Market Indices Inched Their Way to Record Highs Once Again Today..."
–*Schenectady Gazette*, April 17, 1964

During an economic spring season, the "one bucket" approach to managing assets works well. Stocks performed well during the last economic spring season. The Dow Jones Industrial Average was under 200 in 1949, and by 1966, it had risen to about 1,000, an increase of more than 500%! My studies have taught me that this is typical economic spring season behavior for stocks.

The most recent economic summer season in the United States began in 1966 and continued through 1982. During an economic summer season, the "one bucket" approach to managing assets will fail.

As we described earlier, during an economic summer season, an economy sees an increase in the currency supply, which leads to inflation. During summer, private sector debt levels are relatively low. Gold prices reach a significant peak at the end of the summer period. Interest rates rise rapidly and peak at the end of the summer season. Stocks are under pressure and decline through the period, reaching a low at the end of the summer cycle.

Here are some headlines from the most recent economic summer season in the United States:

"Stock Market Turns Downward"
– *The Evening Independent*, February 4, 1975

"Ford to Warn of Inflation Danger"
– *The Age*, June 28, 1976

"President Ends Flow of Gold to Foreign Nations"
– *Los Angeles Times*, August 16, 1971

"Gold Prices Skyrocket 'Out of Sight'"
– *St. Petersburg Times*, September 18, 1979

Stocks perform poorly in an economic summer season, and the last economic summer season was no exception to this rule. The Standard & Poor's 500 began the summer season at a level of between 90 and 100 in 1967 and finished the summer season at about the same level in 1982. For those fifteen years, point to point, stocks provided the same approximate annual return as money under the mattress. During this summer season, stocks also experienced their largest correction since the 1930s, with a decline of nearly 50% from the peak to the trough.

Gold, on the other hand, as one would expect in a summer season, performed much better than stocks. Prior to 1971, the price of gold was fixed at $35 per ounce; but after the link between the US dollar and gold was broken, by 1980, gold prices peaked at about $850 per ounce, a gain of more than 2,300%!

The most recent autumn season in the United States has predictably followed the patterns of the prior three economic autumn seasons that occurred in US history. The economic autumn season is a time of prosperity; however, during autumn, debt slowly rises to unsustainable levels. During an economic autumn season, the "one bucket" approach to managing finances once again performs well, as we'll soon see.

The easy money policies of the 1980s began in earnest after the stock market decline of 1987. Then, just appointed Federal Reserve Chairman Alan Greenspan decided to "provide liquidity" to the economy by reducing the Fed Funds interest rate from 7.5% to 7%.[6] By reducing interest rates, as we discussed in Chapter 2, the Federal Reserve is attempting to boost the economy by using the money throttle, creating more currency by having money move faster through the fractionalized banking system.

Greenspan did raise the Fed Funds interest rate shortly thereafter to try to cool the economy. By 1989, the Fed Funds rate was, once again, back over 9%. But then came the recession of 1990 to 1992. In response, Greenspan reduced interest rates to as low as 3%. However, from mid-1991 through early 2000, the Fed Funds rate never went higher than 5.75%.[7] This cheap credit and easy money allowed the debt bubble to build to unsustainable levels.

The most recent autumn season that led to the current economic winter season was very similar to the prior autumn seasons, with one exception: Debt levels in today's autumn season are much higher than in prior autumn seasons.

Autumn sees stocks do well; however, once the economic season turns to winter and deflation kicks in, stocks do poorly.

Just as occurred in prior winter seasons, as I've already stated, I expect to ultimately see deflation emerge as the dominant economic force unless the Federal Reserve prints massive amounts of currency again and further denigrates the US dollar.

While we can't predict the policy response of the Federal Reserve, we can work to protect our nest eggs and potentially prosper by using the "two bucket" approach to asset management rather than the traditional "one bucket" approach. We'll discuss this in detail in a later chapter.

These economic seasons have recurred for more than 2,000 years.

A good example of an autumn season that transitioned to winter was in early-eighteenth-century France.

John Law was France's central banker. As you now know, a central banker controls a central bank that can print currency virtually out of thin air.

Law was not French but Scottish, having been born in Edinburgh in 1671. He was born into the money business, as his father was a successful banker and goldsmith. Law began working in these trades as an apprentice at the age of 14, and, at the age of 17, began working full time in the family business when his father suddenly passed away.

Law, always popular with the ladies, and now with his family's estate under his control, set off for London, where he learned how to be a successful gambler, which was not a surprising decision for a wealthy 17-year-old. Unfortunately for Law, his gambling and womanizing led to him being challenged to a duel, which he accepted. Law won the duel, killing his challenger. As a result of his role in the duel, Law was sentenced to be hanged. However, with some help from some friends in high places, he managed to escape the death penalty during the appeals process.

Law was an interesting character, to say the least. For the next several years, Law made his living gambling. As a result of this gambling lifestyle, he began to have regular contact with the Duc d'Orleans, who was also an avid gambler. Somewhat surprisingly, even though he led a high-roller kind of life, there were some signs that Law wanted to do more with his life; he wanted to be more significant. Out of the blue, Law began to publish some serious pieces on economics and became very interested in the financing of trade. The Duc thought highly enough of Law to listen to Law's views on trade and finance.

At about this time, Louis XIV of France was dying. While Louis was well regarded during his reign, after his death, he left a mixed legacy due to the size of the national debt that he left to his heir, Louis XV, who was only 7 years old at the time he took the throne. Due to the new king's young age, the Duc d' Orleans was appointed as regent. The first and most pressing problem that the newly appointed regent faced was the huge amount of debt accumulated by the now deceased king.

The Duc made the same decision politicians have made for centuries—he decided to print currency. Because paper currency was not yet in use at the time, the Duc printed currency by debasing the coins used as currency. Newly minted coins were made with a precious metal content that was 20% less than previously issued coins. This was the eighteenth-century equivalent of currency printing. French citizens, recognizing that the older coins were more valuable, began to hoard them. In response, the state passed a law that made hoarding the old coins illegal and punishable by imprisonment. There were also rewards offered to those who blew the whistle on coin hoarders.

Things were going south in a hurry, and that's when Law arrived on the scene. Law was granted a bank and put in charge of the management of royal revenues. He was also given the authority to issue paper currency. The paper currency would be secured by the royal revenues and the land owned by the kingdom.

Law's bank began to print paper currency. Initially, Law guaranteed that the paper currency could be exchanged for the coin (composed of precious metal) that was being issued at the time the paper currency was introduced. This made the paper currency more popular than the coins that were circulating at the time, because it was easier to use than coins. By introducing the paper currency in this manner, Law was able to collect most of the country's precious metal, leaving mostly paper currency circulating. Law calculated that printing more currency would help get the French economy moving again.

Next, Law convinced the Duc to grant him a monopoly on France's Mississippi trade. The French had a colony stretching from the mouth of the Mississippi River all the way north into parts of what is now Canada. In France, Law created a company called the Mississippi Company, which exclusively controlled all trade in the colony for twenty-five years. Law now had control of the coinage, paper currency, and trade with the New World.

Law began to sell stock in the Mississippi Company to raise capital, promising investors a share in a company that controlled trade in a new world abundant with silver and gold. The shares in the company were sold for cash or state bonds, which was a very smart move by Law. State bonds were nothing more than government debt, and there was plenty of that. Now an investor could trade government debt for equity in the Mississippi Company.

Here is why that's important. A bond is a loan, while a share of stock is an ownership position in a company. A bond is typically secured by the assets of the issuer or the entity to which an investor loaned money, while a share of stock is simply a stake in the company. If a stockholder owns stock in a profitable company, he may share in those profits in the form of dividends. By contrast, if the company goes broke, the stockholder may lose his investment. Many investors in France traded these bonds, or loans to the government, for an equity or ownership position in the new company, essentially forgiving the loan that the investor had made to the government. This scheme, devised by Law, helped the French government erase a lot of debt. It was the same exact strategy utilized by Alexander Hamilton eighty years later to erase US government debt when Hamilton convinced

President Washington to establish a central bank that could print paper money.

The Mississippi Company became immensely popular, and speculation with the company's stock was rampant.

Each time there was a new stock offering in the company, the stock was issued at a higher price than at the prior issue. The French public was literally fighting for the right to exchange state bills (government debt) for shares in the Mississippi Company. Currency printing in France's autumn season led to a price bubble in stock prices, typical of an economic autumn season.

The currency printing continued.

It seemed that prosperity was everywhere. Paris was booming. High-end luxury items were sold before they hit the shelves. Real estate values went through the roof. Rents skyrocketed, and the Mississippi Company stock just kept on rising, increasing over 1,900% in just one year! A bubble had been created the same way that bubbles are always created—through easy credit. Yet, in the midst of a bubble, few recognized that the bubble existed. It was France's autumn season.

The Duc saw what prosperity had been created through the printing of currency, and he was a happy guy. He reasoned that if some currency printing had produced these results, then more currency printing would produce even better results. The Duc went over Law's head and ordered more currency printing.

However, as also always happens, some of the smarter French citizens began to get nervous due to the large amount of currency printing. One of the first of the French citizens to take action was a nobleman who sent three wagonloads of paper currency to Law's bank to demand payment in the coins containing precious metals.

The nobleman was paid, but after being advised that he'd upset the Duc, he returned two of the wagons of coins and took back the paper currency. This was enough to allow some of the other smart Frenchmen to see the light: This paper currency system was highly suspect, and the speculative bubble might be close to bursting. More and more French citizens started to cash in their paper currency, exchanging it for coins. Some smart French citizens, fearing the government, began to ship coins, bullion, and jewels to other countries.

The run on the bank for the coins containing precious metals continued, forcing the French parliament to take action. The parliament issued a law that stated that the coins would carry only 95% of the value of paper currency. It didn't work. The public didn't buy it, and the run on the bank for coins continued.

Law had no choice but to abolish coins as a medium of exchange. The French currency was now a fiat currency since the link between paper currency and precious metals was eliminated. Law, in the early eighteenth century, did what President Nixon did in 1971 when the US dollar became a fiat currency.

Law also made it illegal to own gold (like Franklin Roosevelt would do later in the United States during the Great Depression). He closed borders and sent instructions to coach houses to refuse fresh horses to anyone traveling out of the country until their bags were inspected. There were substantial fines for violating these rules, and these fines were shared with the whistleblowers who informed the authorities about these violations.

It wasn't long before the French monetary system collapsed, making Law the most hated man in France. Fortunately for him, he escaped to the city of Venice.

Gold and silver were once again used in commerce after the bubble burst, and it would be eighty years before the French introduced paper currency again. It's no surprise that the timing of the reintroduction of paper currency took eighty years since that's when France entered her next economic autumn season.

The pattern is clear.

Loose money policies lead to debt excesses, which, in turn, lead to an economic winter season when excess debt has to be purged from the system. As we have discussed at length, this pattern has repeated itself time and time again throughout history.

We've discussed the fact that most money today is debt. When debt is purged from the system via nonpayment, the money supply contracts, which is the textbook definition of deflation.

Inflation can only occur if money is added to the financial system via currency printing faster than money leaves the financial system through defaults and the nonpayment of debt.

To illustrate this economic truth, let's look at the case of Weimar, Germany, after World War I.

Germany hoped that it would quickly win the war and reap the bounty from the nations it conquered, which, to the government, justified the use of the printing press to fund the war.

A speedy victory in 1914 had been both hoped for and expected. A fast victory, the German government rationalized, justified taking temporary and even outrageous liberties with the known laws of finance. So the currency printing began.

It didn't take too long for this currency printing to create inflation. However, during the war, the German government used extensive propaganda to attempt to hide the inflation from the population, and it censored information heavily.

Every German stock exchange was closed for the duration of the war, so the effect of Reichsbank (the German central bank that was printing money) policies on stocks was unknown. Further, foreign exchange rates were not published, and only those in contact with neutral markets, such as Amsterdam or Zurich, could guess what was going on. Only when the war was over, when censorship stopped, did it become clear to all that Germany had already met an economic disaster nearly as ugly as her military one.

Due to the economy, many German soldiers began to desert the military. A German newspaper attributed Germany's loss of the war partly to the fact that men were abandoning the front to return home and support their families. With rapidly rising inflation, it was impossible to make ends meet on military pay.

To make things worse, the Treaty of Versailles, which ended the war, imposed huge reparations on Germany. The payment demands made of Germany were so large that Germany could never realistically pay with "honest" money.

The implications of these demands for the German economy were enormous. The German army had to be reduced to 25% of its size, which meant that over 250,000 men were suddenly added to the labor force, increasing the rate of unemployment. The central bank began currency printing in earnest to attempt to stimulate the economy and bring down the unemployment rate.

Inflation set in.

By September 1920, prices were twelve times as high as they had been before the war. By the autumn of 1920, the strains on the economy in the wake of the war were apparent, but employment was still fairly strong. Nevertheless, prices were rising as a direct result of this money printing. Food had accounted for half the family budget immediately after the war, but now nearly three-quarters of any family's income was spent on it. The food for a family of four persons, which cost 60 marks a week in April 1919, cost 198 marks by September 1920, and 230 marks by November 1920. Certain items, such as lard, ham, tea, and eggs, rose to between thirty and forty times the prewar price.

On the bright side, in contrast to Austria, the official unemployment figure was low, and only 375,000 people were on the dole.

Faced with a bill that it could not pay from a war it couldn't afford, Germany continued currency printing at an even faster pace.

The lower and middle classes in Germany were experiencing economic hardship, and the wealthy in Germany were spending money like crazy in order to avoid high taxes. The class divide in Germany began to widen.

The straw that broke the back of the proverbial camel came in August of 1921 when a political assassination sent the German mark plunging.

The assassination undermined any remaining confidence that the German economy might be allowed to recover. Bankers from Switzerland, Italy, and Germany concluded that it was impossible for Germany to continue her reparation payments and that, sooner or later, she would have to declare herself bankrupt, followed (they thought) by France and then Italy. The mark, at 310 to the British pound in mid-August, had sped downward to over 400 by mid-September and was still going down.

Germans everywhere were doing everything they could to convert their marks into other currencies. Goods were flying off the shelves of shops as people tried to protect themselves against the falling value of the currency.

However, a conference of the Allied Powers over reparations in December of 1921 offered Germany a glimmer of hope. The Allied Powers were finally realizing that holding Germany to the following year's reparation payments was unrealistic. This led to a surge in the mark.

But regardless of the politics, the economic realities of currency printing resurfaced. By Christmas 1921, ordinary Germans were feeling the squeeze of inflation.

By the end of 1921, workers had lost so much faith in the government that many just stopped voting. The economic hardships brought about by inflation were evident in everyday prices.

Owners of large industrial conglomerates benefited from the inflation, so they constantly reminded the populace that amid the economic chaos, employment was still very high.

It didn't take long for the cost of basic staples to become out of reach for German consumers as the mark plunged. A liter of milk, which had cost 7 marks in April 1922 and 16 marks in August, cost 26 marks by mid-September. Beer had climbed from 5.60 marks a liter to 18 and then to 30. A single egg, 3.60 marks in April, now cost 9 marks. In only nine months, the weekly bill for an identical food basket had risen from 370 marks to 2,615 marks.

The soaring inflation led to currency chaos, and many entities began to issue their own forms of money. Large industrial concerns began to pay their workmen partly in notes and partly in coupons of their own, which were accepted by local tradesmen on the understanding that they would be redeemed within a very short time. Cities also started to issue their own currencies, aware that any delay in receiving their pay packets would dangerously aggravate workers, whose main concern was to spend them before they depreciated.

At 35,000 to the British pound at Christmas in 1922, the mark fell, and at the end of January 1923, it touched 227,500, which was well over 50,000 to the US dollar.

At the end of September of 1923, the German Chancellor declared a state of emergency and put Germany under military rule. Finally, in November of 1923, the German government took action to stabilize the currency. The German government set up the Rentenbank to issue a new currency, the rentenmark, which would be backed by land and industrial goods. The rentenmark finally stabilized the German currency.

The next month, in December, the food shortages of the summer finally began to recede. Finally, a month after the rentenmark was introduced, everyday Germans were able to feed themselves again.

However, after a recovery in 1924, a whole new crisis hit Germany in 1925—mass unemployment. The strengthened currency and subsiding hyperinflationary pressures once again brought German industry to its knees, as several firms plunged into bankruptcy and unemployment soared.

It was at this time that Hitler began to rise to power.

Currency printing to solve a debt problem failed. Once currency printing failed, the consequences of debt excesses still had to be dealt with. Time and time again in history, politicians of many generations have tried to solve the same problem using the same policies, and the end result has always been the same.

This time can be no different.

Thomas Jefferson understood this from his study of history. His observation of more than two hundred years ago seems eerily prophetic today:

If the American people ever allow private banks to control the issue of their currency, first by inflation, then by deflation, the banks and corporations that will grow up around them will deprive the people of all property until their children wake up homeless on the continent their fathers conquered.

[1] Source: http://www.landandfreedom.org/ushistory/us8.htm

[2] Source: http://www.publicbookshelf.com/public_html/The_Great_Republic_By_the_Master_Historians_Vol_III/thepanic_ce.html

[3] Source: http://www.publicbookshelf.com/public_html/The_Great_Republic_By_the_Master_Historians_Vol_III/panicof1_hd.html

[4] Source: https://suite101.com/a/the-financial-crisis-of-the-1870s-a102773

[5] Source: http://www.library.hbs.edu/hc/crises/forgotten.html

[6] Source: http://www.federalreserve.gov/pubs/feds/2007/200713/200713pap.pdf

[7] Source: http://www.newyorkfed.org/markets/statistics/dlyrates/fedrate.html

CHAPTER FOUR

Demographics

The economic winter season in which we find ourselves will not end until enough debt is purged from the system. A study of history confirms this.

In addition to unsustainable debt levels, there is another, less noticeable factor that will be a drag on the economy moving ahead. In a word, this factor is demographics.

Demographics is defined as a study of the changes that occur in large groups of people over a period of time.

The study of demographics is important for understanding future economic growth, particularly in an economy that needs consumers to spend in order for it to be healthy. The US economy is such an economy, with consumer spending comprising 70% of GDP.

GDP, the most common measure of an economy, comprises four elements: consumer spending plus investment plus government spending plus or minus net exports.

The consumer spending component is easily defined: It's consumption by you and me of items such as groceries, clothes, cars, and education. The investment component of GDP is investment in new manufacturing facilities or homes (sales of existing homes are not counted in the investment component of GDP). The government-spending component is also self-explanatory. The final component of GDP is net exports. Since the United States currently imports more than it exports, this component is negative in the GDP calculation.

Since US economic growth is largely dependent on consumer spending, a study of demographics and the spending patterns of various age groups is useful in forecasting future economic growth.

Consumer spending, like economic cycles, is predictable on average by age group.

From the ages of 18 through 22, many in the population are students. Students typically work part-time and spend a lot more money than they make, which is generally not much. The biggest economic decision facing many young adults is whether to do takeout or eat frozen pizza, depending on how wealthy they are feeling. The spending of this age group doesn't boost the economy very much.

From the ages of 22 through 30, consumer spending increases. Many in this group are young and have just gotten married. They may be buying a first or a trade-up car. They are often living in apartments as they enter the workforce for the very first time on a full-time or more permanent basis. While this group participates in the consumer-spending portion of the economy to a greater extent than the 18- to 22-year-olds, they are not the big spenders they'll become when their families start to grow and mature.

The next group contains the 31- to 45-year-olds. Many in this group are buying their first home and maybe even buying a new car for the first time. This group often has growing families with young and teenage children. As any parent knows, caring for children requires money. They need to be fed, clothed, and educated. They need trips to the dentist, doctor, and orthodontist. They want to go to Disney World and summer camps. Basketball clinics and soccer leagues are a part of their lives. Birthdays and Christmas mean presents—often expensive presents—will be purchased. This group spends the second most of any demographic group, helping to boost the consumer-spending-dependent economy.

The next group comprises the 46- to 50-year-olds. This group is the highest spending group on average. A consumer-spending-driven economy depends on this group to a great extent. This crowd may be buying their trade-up home or a second home. They are likely spending money on college tuition and weddings for their children. Many in this group own three or even four cars, as the children are driving and need transportation while they are away at school. These extra cars need to be repaired, washed, and fueled.

The next group is the 51- to 59-year-olds. Their children are through college and (hopefully) independent. They've sold the extra cars, and now that they are empty nesters, they may be thinking about downsizing the house. They are spending less on groceries and fuel. They are past their peak when it comes to their level of consumer spending. They are focused on paying down debts and saving for retirement. As important as it is to save money for retirement, it's not helpful when an economy is as dependent on consumer spending as the US economy is.

Finally, there are those over age 60. This group spends even less than the 51- to 59-year-olds. They may still be saving for retirement or may already be retired. Other than the occasional purchase of a vacation home or a retirement home by some in this group, they don't spend much.

The bottom line for this analysis?

The more of the population that is age 46 to 50 and in their peak spending years, the better it is for the consumer-spending-dependent US economy.

The baby boomers, the largest segment of the US population, were born from 1946 through 1964.[1]

After World War II, in 1946, 3.4 million babies were born—20% more than in 1945. In 1947, 3.8 million babies were born. Then through 1964, more than 4 million babies were born every year. By 1964, the baby boomers numbered over 76 million and made up about 40% of the US population.

By taking the birth year of the baby boomers and adding forty-six to fifty years, we have a rough idea of what percentage of the US population might be at their peak spending years. Those born in 1946 reached their peak spending years in 1992, at about the beginning of the massive autumn season stock bull market. Those born in 1964 reached their peak spending years in 2010. Boomers are now at the stage of life where consumer spending is declining and will decline even further than it already has.

As I stated at the outset of this chapter, that's an additional dose of bad news for the US economy.

The generation that follows the baby boomers is known as Generation X. Generation Xers are defined as US citizens born between 1965 and 1982. There are not nearly as many Generation Xers as there are baby boomers. So, even though Generation Xers are now reaching their peak spending years, there are simply not enough of them to make up for the lack of spending by the baby boomers. Because Generation X numbers are much smaller than baby boomer numbers, consumer spending is declining.

When one looks at the number of births in the United States, one observes the birth rate decline from 1962 through 1975.[2] In 1962, there were about 4.2 million births, and by 1975, there were only about 3.1 million, a decline of more than 26%.

In 1976, the birth rate began to increase, and by 1985, the birth rate hit 3.7 million. By 1989, annual births exceeded 4 million. Americans born in 1976 and continuing through 1992 are considered part of the demographic group known as echo boomers. Taking the birth rates of the echo boomers and adding forty-six years to them has the demographic influences on the US economy turning from negative to positive by the year 2023 and becoming more positive each year through 2036.

If you want a guess as to when the next economic season may change from winter to spring, I'll go with 2023. It will likely take at least that long for private sector debt levels to get low enough for the ugly influences of deflation to subside. At that point in time, the echo boomers will be reaching their peak spending years. It will be time for an economic spring season.

[1] Source: http://www.history.com/topics/baby-boomers

[2] Source: http://nces.ed.gov/programs/projections/projections2020/tables/table_B01.asp?referrer=list

CHAPTER FIVE

Winter Season Investment Forecast

I've always found it amazing that some weather forecasters can be wrong about their forecast more often than they are right and can still keep their jobs.

Many investment forecasters have a far worse track record than weather forecasters, and there are numerous examples to prove this.

Take, for example, the US stock market decline that began in late 2007 and continued through early 2009. Just prior to the stock market decline beginning, and even during the decline, many mainstream commentators, policymakers, and money managers had it wrong—very wrong. Here are some examples:[1]

"Mad Money" Jim Cramer: "Bye-bye bear market, say hello to the bull."

Ken Fisher: "This year will end in the plus column . . . so keep buying."

Ben Bernanke: No "serious failures among large internationally active banks."

Goldman Sachs: "Fear priced into stocks is likely to abate as recession fears fade."

Barney Frank: "Freddie Mac and Fannie Mae are fundamentally sound."

Barron's: "Home prices about to bottom."

***Worth* magazine:** "Emerging markets are the global investors' safe haven."

Bernie Madoff: "It's virtually impossible to violate the rules."

***Kiplinger's*:** "Stock investors should beat the rush to the banks."

Bear Stearns and Lehman Brothers failed after Mr. Bernanke's comments. Freddie and Fannie required government money to remain solvent, and you already know the Bernie Madoff story.

These examples demonstrate that betting your nest egg on a forecast can lead to ruin.

But these examples are not just limited to the most recent major stock market decline. One can go back and look at comments made by commentators, forecasters, and investors prior to the 2001 to 2003 stock market correction and reach the same conclusion.[1] As you read these quotes, remember the stock market peaked in September of 2001 and bottomed in early 2003.

James Glassman, author of *Dow 36,000*: "What is dangerous is for Americans not to be in the market. We're going to reach a point where stocks are correctly priced . . . not a bubble. . . . market is undervalued." (October 1999)

Larry Kudlow, CNBC host: "This correction will run its course until the middle of the year. . . . not even Greenspan can stop the Internet economy." (February 2000)

Jim Cramer: "SUNW probably has the best near-term outlook of any company I know." (September 2000)

Lehman's Jeffrey Applegate: "The bulk of the correction is behind us, so now is the time to be offensive, not defensive." (December 2000)

Alan Greenspan: "The 3- to 5-year earnings projections of more than a thousand analysts . . . have generally held firm. Such expectations, should they persist, bode well for continued capital deepening and sustained growth." (December 2000)

Suze Orman: "The QQQ, they're a buy. They may go down, but if you dollar-cost average, where you put money every single month into them . . . in the long run, it's the way to play the Nasdaq." (January 2001)

Maria Bartiromo, CNBC reporter: "The individual out there is actually not throwing money at things that they do not understand, and is actually using the news and using the information out there to make smart decisions." (March 2001)

Goldman Sachs's Abby Joseph Cohen: "The time to be nervous was a year ago. The S&P then was overvalued, it's now undervalued." (April 2001)

Lou Dobbs, CNN Host: "Let me make it very clear. I'm a bull, on the market, on the economy. And let me repeat, I am a bull." (August 2001)

Larry Kudlow: "The shock therapy of a decisive war will elevate the stock market by a couple thousand points," with Dow 35,000 by 2010. (June 2002)

More recent forecasters and prognosticators have nothing on those commenting prior to the 90% decline in stocks at the onset of the Great Depression. Look at what investors heard around the 1929 crash:

Irving Fisher, Yale Ph.D. in economics: "Stock prices have reached what looks like a permanently high plateau. I do not feel there will be soon if ever a 50 or 60 point break from present levels . . . I expect to see the stock market a good deal higher within a few months." (October 17, 1929, just days before the Crash)

Goodbody market letter in *New York Times*: "We feel that fundamentally Wall Street is sound, and that for people who can afford to pay for them outright, good stocks are cheap at these prices." (October 25, 1929)

***BusinessWeek*:** "The Wall Street crash doesn't mean that there will be any general or serious business depression . . . For six years American business has been diverting a substantial part of its attention, its energies and its resources on the speculative game . . . Now that irrelevant, alien and hazardous adventure is over. Business has come home again, back to its job, providentially unscathed, sound in wind and limb, financially stronger than ever before." (November 2, 1929)

Harvard Economic Society: "A serious depression seems improbable . . . recovery of business next spring, with further improvement in the fall." (November 10, 1929)

Andrew W. Mellon, Treasury Secretary: "I see nothing in the present situation that is either menacing or warrants pessimism . . . I have every confidence that there will be a revival of activity in the spring, and that during this coming year the country will make steady progress." (December 31, 1929)

***Wall Street Journal*:** As the Dow fell from 298 to 41, "Chase National Bank says the current conditions of very easy credit and poor business have always been a buying opportunity in the past. Absolutely confident that any list of good stocks will have good gains by end of 1931 and probably show a profit by end of 1930." (June 1930)

President Herbert Hoover: "The depression is over." (June 1930)

Notice that at every stock market top, leaders and gurus were overly optimistic.

From my experience, stock investors want to believe the optimists, as do the financial professionals who use the "one bucket" approach. No matter how high stocks get in price, stock investors do their best to will them even higher. Stock investors want to believe in a better future, so they devour the happy talk no matter the economic fundamentals.

While no forecast is 100% accurate, overly bullish sentiment is often one sign that a stock market top may have arrived.

There's an old contrarian trading strategy that advises that when the bull is on the cover of all the news magazines, it's time to sell. When the bear is on the cover, it's time to buy.

As the stock market was bottoming in March of 2009, bullish sentiment among stock investors was just 3%.[2] As bullish sentiment bottomed, so did the stock market.

Today, there is no shortage of stock market bulls, although, at this writing the market appears to be very "toppy" and full of volatility.

Another factor worthy of consideration is margin debt levels. Margin debt is debt incurred to buy securities using the securities in a brokerage account as collateral. As the value of securities in an account increases, so does equity in the account. As equity in the account increases, so does borrowing power since an investor with the ability to borrow on margin can borrow up to 50% of his account equity to buy additional stocks.

As stocks rally, more equity is created in a brokerage account, and borrowing power increases. This cycle can feed on itself for a while and even result in more robust stock rallies than may have otherwise occurred without the existence of margin debt. However, as you now know, debt can only increase to a finite level. Once the system's capacity to service debt is reached, debt levels must begin to reverse.

In the case of margin debt, the system's capacity for debt is usually reached at about the same time that stocks peak, and then the margin debt accumulation trend reverses. As stocks decline, equity in a brokerage account declines. As equity declines, margin debt must also decline since the minimum level of equity in a margin account must be 50%. Declining stocks often result in margin calls, which is a demand by a brokerage

FINRA Margin Debt and the S&P 500
Real Values (Adjusted to Present-Day Dollars)

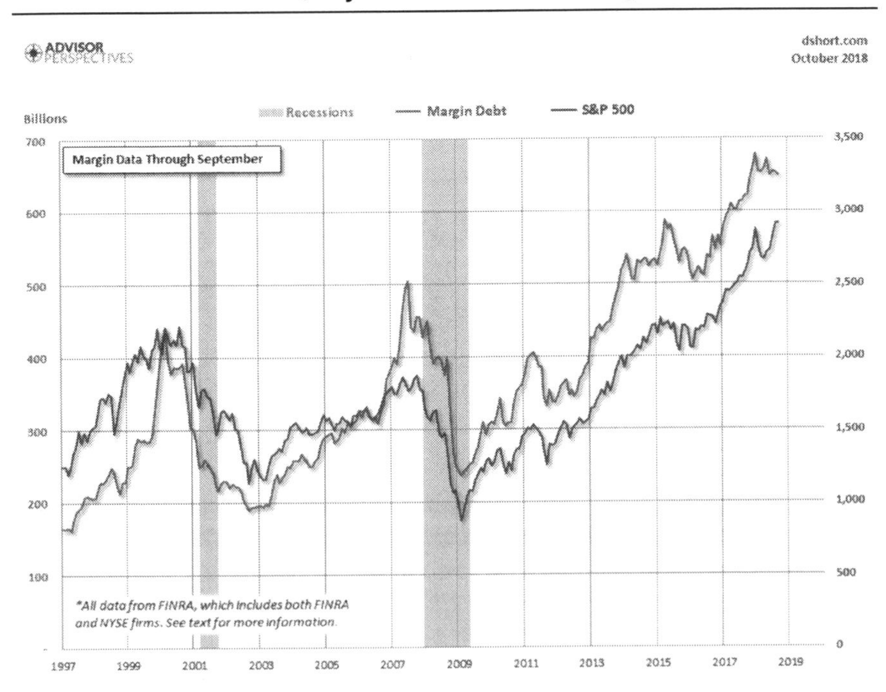

company to sell stocks in order to maintain a minimum level of equity in the brokerage account.

When one examines margin debt levels that existed prior to the declines in the stock market beginning in 2001 and then again in 2007, a pattern is observed.

Take a look at the chart below, illustrating the values of the S&P 500 and margin debt levels.

Notice the high correlation between margin debt levels and the price of stocks. In both 2001 and 2007, margin debt levels began to decline before the stock market began their steep declines.

At the time of this writing, stocks are at still near their all-time highs although signs of a decline are becoming more obvious, and margin debt levels are far higher than in 2001 and 2007. While it is important to note that just because something has happened historically doesn't mean it will happen again, however, this is a red flag that bears further observance.

From an expert perspective, a bullish sentiment perspective, and a margin debt perspective, stocks may be subject to decline from these rather lofty levels. However, in my view, there is a much better way to look at the likely behavior of stocks moving ahead.

Historically speaking, as we've already discussed, whenever private sector debt levels have reached unsustainable levels—like today's—a period of deflation sets in. Stocks don't like deflation; so, at some future point, I am expecting a major decline in stocks that will likely be greater in magnitude than the declines that began in 2001 and 2007.

One of the main reasons I have concluded that a significant stock market decline lies ahead is the current and historical relationship between the price of gold and the price of stocks. Over longer time frames, the price of gold and the price of stocks are inversely correlated. When stock prices are up, gold prices tend to be down, and when gold prices are up, stock prices tend to be down.

Measuring the price of stocks in US dollars, as most do, can lead to a conclusion that is flawed. As we've discussed, the US dollar, along with every other currency being used today, is a fiat currency. Central banks around the world are collectively devaluing currencies in an effort to get an export edge and stimulate their economies.

This currency devaluation has a blurring effect on the price of stocks.

Three Indexes: Percent Change from Their 2000 Peaks

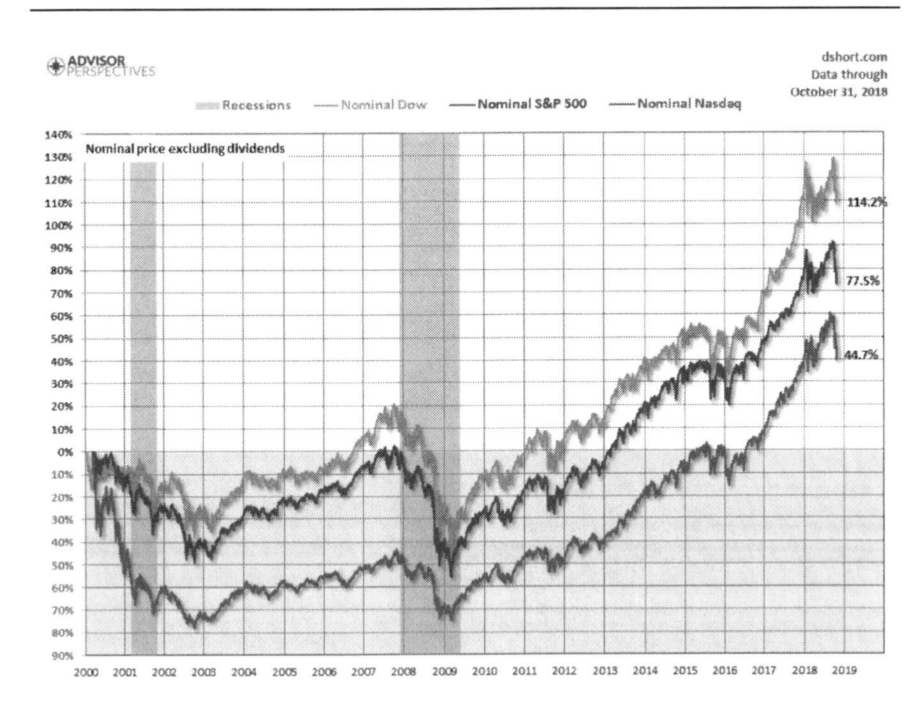

As the US dollar is devalued, not only do consumer prices rise but so does the price of stocks.

Looking at the level of the Dow Jones Industrial Average since 2000, the Dow has nominally increased from about 11,700 to a bit more than 24,000 as of this writing; in other words, about double.

But that's double in nominal terms, not real terms, because the US dollar has lost purchasing power over the past nineteen years. The first chart shows the performance of the three major US stock indices in nominal terms. (The terrific chart was prepared by Jill Mislinski and published at Advisor Perspectives.)

Notice the Dow is up about 114% in nominal terms.

Three "Real" Indexes: Percent Change from Their 2000 Peaks

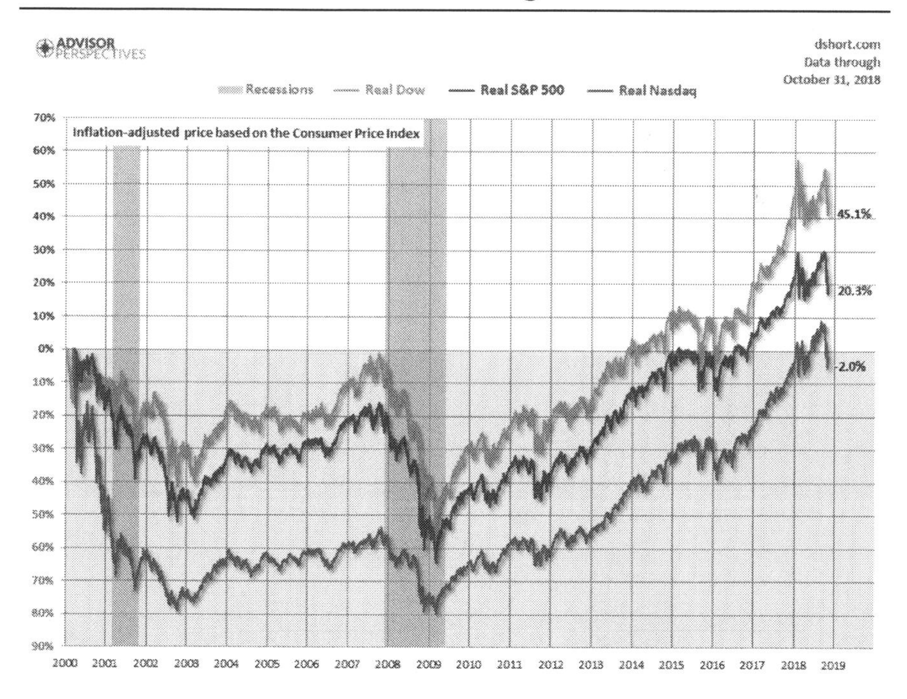

Adjusted for the official inflation rate, the Dow has returned only about 45%, as the second chart illustrates.

If the value of the Dow were adjusted for what might be closer to the real inflation rate rather than the official inflation rate, a different picture emerges.

Using a 5% inflation rate assumption would put the current value of the Dow Jones Industrial Average at about 28,000, a value greater than the current value.

If we assume that the real inflation rate is 5%, that means the Dow has experienced negative growth since the turn of the century.

That is typical of an economic winter season. The metrics of this economic winter season are different from those of many prior winter economic seasons in that all world currencies are fiat currencies and currency devaluation has occurred at a rapid pace.

Arguably, using the US dollar to measure stock market performance may not be the best metric over the last eighty years. The US dollar has been losing purchasing power since 1933 when then President Franklin Roosevelt ordered that all Americans turn in their gold to allow the government to print currency to attempt to alleviate the symptoms of the Great Depression.

This decline continued when President Richard Nixon eliminated the last link between the US dollar and gold in 1971. The decline has accelerated since.

Prior to 1933, going all the way back to 1791, the US dollar's relative value was fairly stable since, for much of that time frame, the US dollar was exchangeable for gold at a fixed rate. From 1791 through 1933, point to point, there was zero price inflation. The US dollar bought about the same amount of goods and services in 1933 as it did in 1791.

The Greenback's Purchasing Power

This log scale chart of the purchasing power of the dollar begins with an index value of 100 at the passage of the Mint Act of 1792. The solid lines present periods when the dollar was convertible into a specific quantity of gold, and the fluctuations represent changes in the purchasing power of gold. The dotted lines present periods when the dollar was not pegged to gold, during and after the War of 1812, the Civil War, World War I and World War II. There was limited convertibility from 1945 to 1971, but the dollar lost purchasing power during the period. The last link between the U.S. currency and gold was cut in 1971 and the loss of purchasing power accelerated. By 2004, the dollar had lost more than 92% of its original purchasing power.

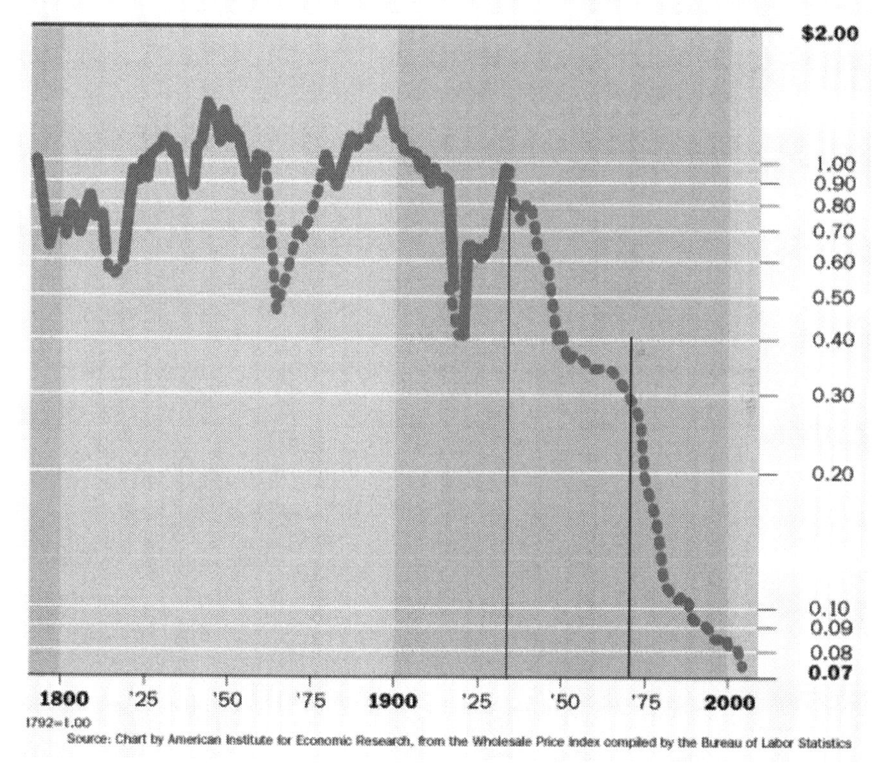

Source: Chart by American Institute for Economic Research, from the Wholesale Price Index compiled by the Bureau of Labor Statistics

However, since 1933, as the chart (reprinted from Chapter Two) illustrates, the US dollar has lost more than 95% of its purchasing power.

Notice also that during the 142-year period from 1791 through 1933, there were three major exceptions to this constant purchasing power rule. In each case, due to easy money policies, an economic autumn season resulted in private sector debt reaching unsustainable levels.

The most obvious of the three exceptions was the decline in the purchasing power of the US dollar preceding the Roaring Twenties, the economic autumn season that preceded the economic winter season we now know as the Great Depression. Easy money policies during the autumn season of the 1920s led to a feel-good prosperity illusion, which is typical of an economic autumn season.

As we've already discussed, the economic autumn season of the 1920s had private sector debt rising to unsustainable levels as a result of easy money policies.

As we've demonstrated, this subcycle has repeated itself time after time historically, both in the United States and in other countries in every century.

The chart also shows that, during the economic autumn season of the 1860s, the purchasing power of the US dollar declined by a little less than half. In order to finance the Civil War, President Lincoln urged Congress to change the backing of the US dollar from gold to government debt, resulting in an expansion and, consequently, a devaluation of the US dollar.

The third exception to the constant purchasing power rule was the economic autumn season of the 1820s and 1830s. The United States established a central bank that could print paper money after the War of 1812, and the easy money policies that followed created an economic autumn season, which was followed by an economic winter season that kicked off with the Panic of 1837.

If we conclude that the US dollar is a poor way to measure stock market performance, given the massive devaluation of the currency, we need to use an alternative measurement that is more constant. Since there was zero price inflation from 1791 through 1933, when the US dollar was directly linked to gold, we might use gold as an alternative measure of stock market performance.

The chart below illustrates the value of the Dow Jones Industrial Average when priced in gold. The values on the chart are calculated by dividing the value of the Dow Jones Industrial Average by the price of gold.

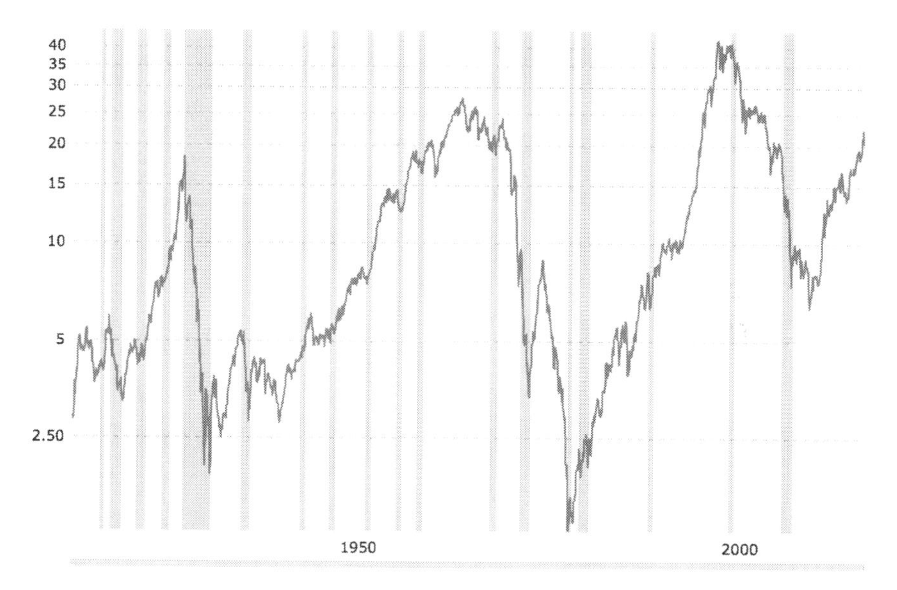

In 1929, at the peak of the stock market just prior to the onset of the Great Depression, it took 18.4 ounces of gold to buy the Dow Jones Industrial Average. In 1932, after the Dow's massive decline, it took only about 2 ounces of gold to buy the Dow. During this time frame, the "one bucket" approach to managing money performed dismally.

At the end of the economic spring season in 1966, the Dow-to-gold ratio stood at about 28, meaning that it took about 28 ounces of gold to buy the Dow. This time frame was good for the "one bucket" approach to managing money.

By the time the economic summer season ended in 1982, the Dow-to-gold ratio dropped to 1. Had you used the "one bucket" management approach during this time frame, your results would have been poor.

At the end of the economic autumn season in 1999, the Dow-to-gold ratio was over 40—a terrific time for investors using the "one bucket" approach.

Dow Jones Industrials/Gold

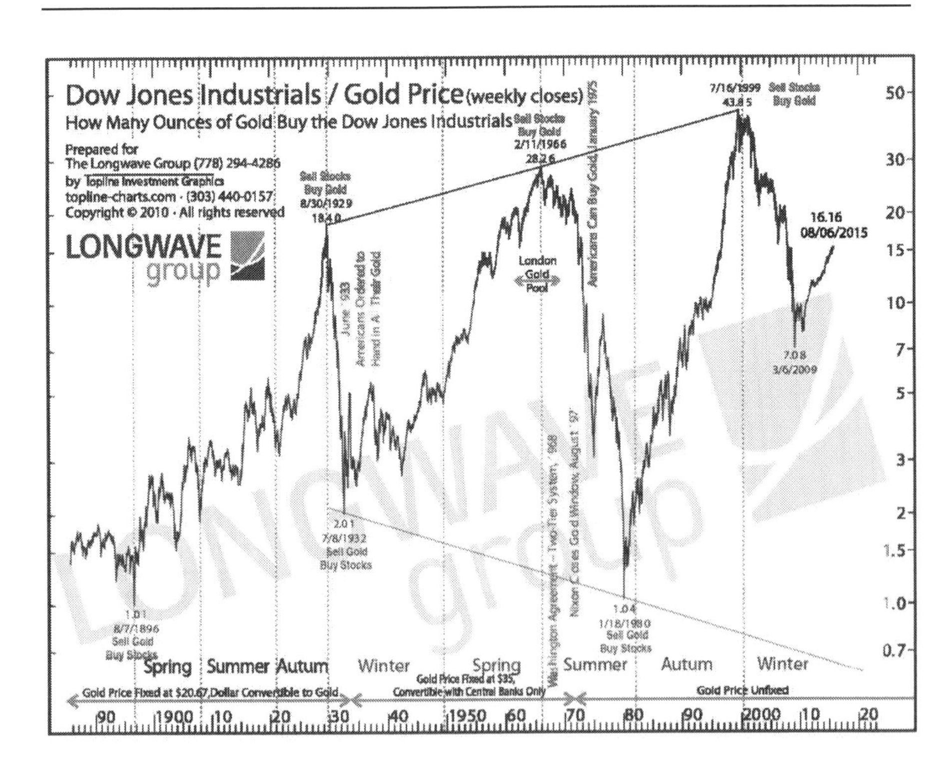

As of this writing, the Dow-to-gold ratio is hovering under 20.

I fully expect that by the end of this economic winter season, we will see the Dow-to-gold ration decline to at least 2, but more likely 1.

The chart below, courtesy of the Longwave Group, shows why I have reached this conclusion.

The chart shows the Dow-to-gold ratio going back to the 1880s. Since 1933, when President Roosevelt made it illegal to own gold, note how each peak in the Dow-to-gold ratio has been higher than the prior peak, and each low in the ratio has been lower than the prior low. I expect that the next low will likely continue this trend.

So what does this mean in terms of the future level of the Dow?

Based on the 130 years of history illustrated on the Dow-to-gold chart, the future level of the Dow will have to be much lower than it is today. Assuming a Dow-to-gold ratio of 1, this might have the Dow at 3,000 and the price of gold at $3,000 per ounce.

Assuming a ratio of 2 at the stock market bottom, this might see gold at $2,000 per ounce or $2,500 per ounce and the Dow at 4,000 or 5,000.

The numbers are hard to predict, but I believe a ratio of 2 or 1 is highly likely.

This is why I believe that the "two bucket" approach to investing will be vitally important moving ahead. Using the "two bucket" approach, you may be able to not only protect yourself but even profit.

[1] Source: Market Watch, July 6, 2013, "Why optimism is your worst investing enemy," by Paul B. Farrell, http://www.marketwatch.com/story/why-optimism-is-your-worst-investing-enemy-2013-07-06?pagenumber=2

[2] Source: http://seekingalpha.com/article/1930291-new-records-in-bullish-stock-market-sentiment

CHAPTER SIX

How Asset Classes May Perform in Each Economic Season

In this chapter, we'll begin to explore how different asset classes perform in each economic season and look at some asset classes that many "one bucket" financial professionals would call nontraditional.

Let me once again state my belief that many stockbrokers and financial professionals will fail their clients and destroy nest eggs in this winter season because of their "one bucket" approach to managing assets. These "one bucket" financial professionals limit the asset classes they use in portfolios to just two types of assets—stocks and bonds.

While we have discussed the difference between stocks and bonds in a prior chapter, I will define them again to frame this discussion.

Stocks are ownership shares in a company. When you own a share of stock, you own a piece of a business. If the business is profitable and grows, your stock may become more valuable. If the business fails, you could lose your entire investment.

Bonds are loans made to companies. When you own a bond issued by a business, you have loaned that business money. Businesses issue bonds or get loans from investors for any number of reasons: perhaps to build a new factory, to invest in equipment, or to retire old debt. Bondholders' interests are secured by the assets of the business. If a business fails, bondholders may recover some or all of their investment, depending on the assets of the company.

As you now know, history tells us that it would be wise to use more than just the two traditional asset classes typically recommended by many "one bucket" financial professionals during an economic winter season.

A review of prior economic cycles and which asset classes performed best during each economic cycle shows that this has been the case.

(SINDU) Dow Jones Industrial Average

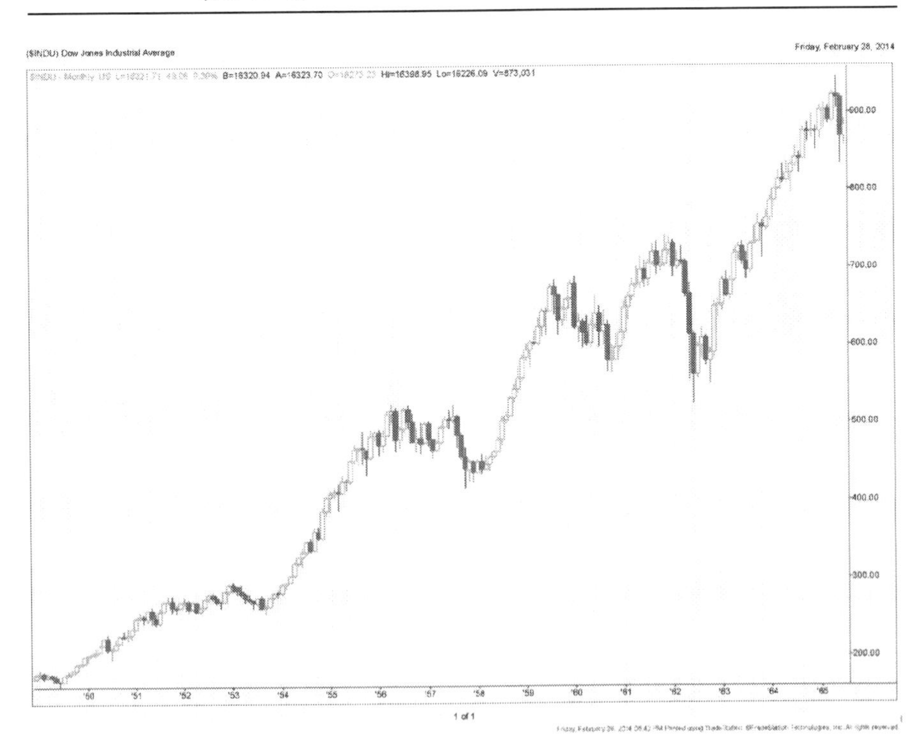

Take, for example, the economic spring cycle from 1949 through 1966.

Remember our definition of the economic spring cycle. The economic spring is characterized by a gradual increase in business and employment. Consumer confidence gradually increases. Consumer prices begin a gradual increase compared to levels seen during the previous cycle (the winter cycle). Stock prices rise and reach a peak at the end of the spring cycle. Credit gradually expands, and at the beginning of the spring cycle, overall debt levels are low.

The chart below shows how stocks did during this cycle. The chart, a monthly chart of the Dow Jones Industrial Average, shows that the Dow began the spring cycle at a level of about 150 and ended the spring cycle at a level of about 900; that's about a 600% increase!

In an economic spring cycle, bonds tend to perform poorly given that interest rates rise during a spring cycle.

The "one bucket" approach to managing assets using only stocks and bonds will perform relatively well in an economic spring environment. The price gains in stocks may more than offset any declines in bond prices.

But what about nontraditional asset classes, such as precious metals and cash? How do these asset classes perform in an economic spring cycle?

Precious metals, whose price typically moves inversely to stocks over longer time frames, tend to perform poorly during an economic spring cycle.

Cash is always a positive asset. It's just that, in some economic cycles, it's more positive than in others. In an economic spring cycle, when interest rates are rising, cash accounts tend to become more positive as the cycle progresses.

In an economic summer season, stocks do poorly. During the summer season from 1967 through 1982, stocks experienced almost no gain from point to point. That's fifteen years during which stocks did nothing.

If you did own stocks during this time frame, as the S&P 500 chart illustrates, you not only experienced almost no gain over this fifteen-year time frame, you also experienced a lot of volatility.

In an economic summer season, bonds also tend to do poorly since interest rates are rising.

(SINX) S&P 500 Index

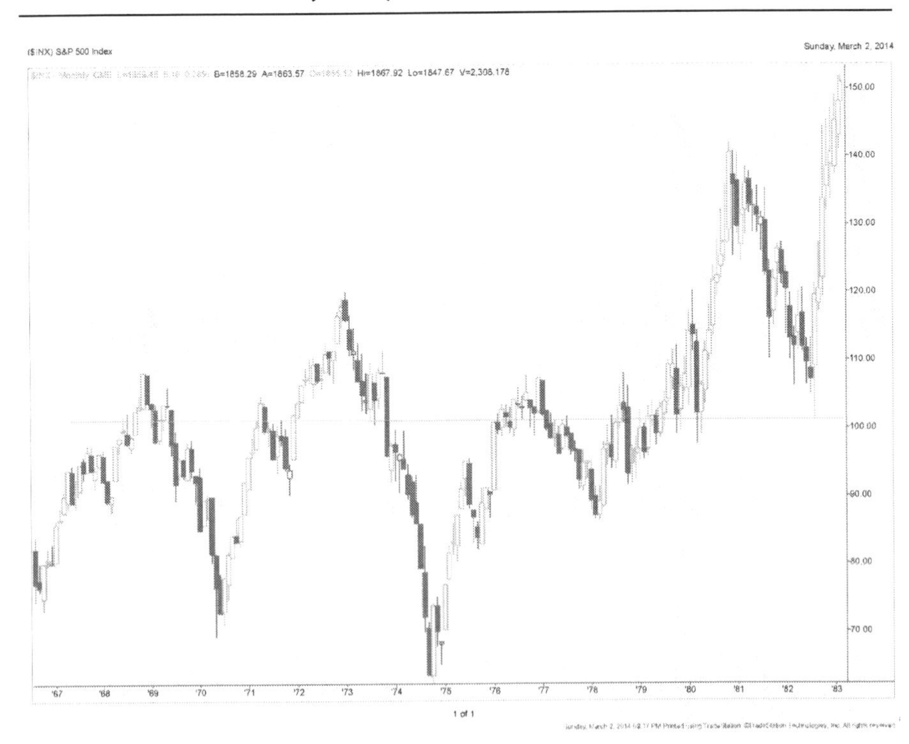

The "one bucket" approach to managing assets in an economic summer season using only stocks and bonds is simply disastrous.

Remember our definition of an economic summer season. The economy sees an increase in the money supply, which leads to inflation. Gold prices reach a significant peak at the end of the summer period. Interest rates rise rapidly and peak at the end of the summer season. Stocks are under pressure and decline through the period, reaching a low at the end of the summer cycle.

During the summer season, cash continues to perform well. Given the environment of rising interest rates and given that cash accounts respond immediately to rising interest rates, cash accounts are even more positive in an economic summer season than they were in the spring season.

Gold is the king of all assets in an economic summer season. Gold, arguably the granddaddy of inflation hedges, does well as the money supply expands during the summer cycle as overall debt levels are low.

In 1971, when then President Richard Nixon eliminated the last link between gold and the US dollar, gold was being sold for $35 per ounce. By the end of the summer season, in 1980, gold reached a record high price of $850 per ounce, making it the number-one performing asset of the economic summer season.

However, during the autumn season, the outlook changes significantly for traditional and nontraditional asset classes of precious metals and cash.

The autumn season that followed the summer season saw stocks and bonds do well, while gold performed very poorly.

Let me remind you of our autumn season definition. During autumn, money is plentiful and gold prices fall, reaching a gold bear market low by the end of the autumn season. During autumn, there is a massive stock bull market and much speculation. Financial fraud is prevalent, and real estate prices rise significantly due to speculation. Debt levels are astronomical. Consumer confidence is at an all-time high due to high stock prices, high real estate prices, and plentiful jobs.

Gold prices during the last autumn season fell to less than $280 per ounce, making gold the worst-performing investment during the autumn season time frame from 1982 through 2000.

Cash accounts, while still positive, were not as positive as

(SINX) S&P 500 Index

during the prior economic summer season. Interest rates on cash accounts fell as the autumn season progressed.

Stocks did extremely well during the autumn season, as the chart illustrates. Notice the S&P 500 began the summer season at a level of about 150 and ended the autumn season about 1,000% higher!

Massively positive stock action is typical of an economic autumn environment. As private sector debt levels build from consumption, the economy seems to be prosperous, and stocks respond accordingly.

Bonds did well during this time frame. Interest rates, which were at record highs at the end of the summer season, began to fall as the autumn season began and continued to fall throughout the entire autumn season. It was a massive bond bull market.

The "one bucket" approach to money management works best in an economic autumn environment.

The winter season that follows the economic autumn season sees the tide change once again for traditional asset classes.

Stocks and bonds do poorly, interest rates rise, and deflationary trends kick in as debt is purged from the system. Gold does well, and cash, although yields are low at the beginning of the winter season, stays positive, with yields increasing as the economic winter season passes.

Our winter season definition sees economies experiencing a crippling credit crisis with money becoming scarce. Financial institutions are in trouble. There are unprecedented bankruptcies at the personal, corporate, and government levels. There is a credit crunch, and interest rates rise. There is an international monetary crisis. There are pension funding problems, and the price of gold and gold-related equities rise.

When reading the winter season investment forecast, it's important to remember that markets never go straight up or straight down. An economic season lasts for more than a decade, often two decades. Over a fifteen-to-twenty-year time frame, even asset classes that do poorly during an overall economic season will have some good years.

As we discussed in Chapter Five, we expect the Dow-to-gold ratio to reach a level of 2 at a minimum, with 1 being more likely. This is consistent with the definition of a winter season and with the performance of these asset classes in prior economic winter seasons.

Given that we are currently in the midst of an economic winter season, the symptoms of which have been temporarily suppressed by the money printing of the Federal Reserve, how do you potentially protect yourself and your assets moving ahead?

This is the topic of the next chapter.

CHAPTER SEVEN

Navigating and Prospering in the Economic Winter Season

If we could predict policy response by the Federal Reserve, it would be fairly easy to figure out where to put your assets.

But policy response can change rapidly.

While the Federal Reserve has "tapered" or stopped the money printing as of this writing and begun to raise interest rates, we don't know what the actions of the Fed might be if the stock market were to suddenly decline.

Will the Fed "take another swing" at jump-starting the markets by increasing the rate at which money is printed? And, if money is printed in great new quantities, will inflation rear its head?

Or will it stay the course and preserve the integrity of the US dollar by continuing to slow and ultimately stop the money printing? If this is the course of action pursued by the Fed, history teaches us that the economy will have to suffer through deflation, which is the result of debt being purged from the system.

We've examined many historical examples of each policy response in prior chapters.

In every historical example of inflation as a result of money printing when debt levels were high, the inflation was followed by deflation. Weimar, Germany, and John Law's France are great examples of this failed policy.

If money printing stops more quickly, deflation will commence sooner.

There are modern-day examples of each of these outcomes.

The country of Greece was in a deflationary depression for many years. Policymakers in Greece can only choose the first two policy responses from the list of three I introduced in a prior chapter.

Choice one:	Raise taxes
Choice two:	Cut spending

Because Greece is a member of the eurozone, printing money is not an option. Greek politicians could only raise taxes or cut spending to deal with their deficit spending. And that's what they did.

The result of cutting spending and raising taxes has been a success, fiscally speaking. The Greek government deficit was cut from 15.6% in 2009 to 4.1% in 2013.[1] That's good progress, but it has not been without pain—deflationary pain.

Greece, since the financial crisis, has lost more than 25% of its GDP.[2] That's an economic decline along the lines of the decline experienced by the United States during the Great Depression.

Personal income levels in Greece were in free fall since the beginning of the economic contraction. That's deflation, pure and simple. Wages in the private sector in Greece have fallen 30% over a four-year period beginning in 2010. The same generation of Greeks who grew accustomed to cheap credit when Greece joined the eurozone in 2002 had to adjust and learn to live on far less.

The Greek unemployment rate reached 27.5%.[3] Youth unemployment in Greece went over 55%.

As debt was purged from the system, Greece has now recovered some, although economic growth is still tepid at best, with growth projections for 2019 remaining below 2%.

At the same time, on the same planet, the country of Venezuela is experiencing massive inflation and economic turmoil.

Basic staples, such as milk, flour, sugar, cooking oil, and butter, are nearly impossible to find.[4] People have taken to the streets to protest high inflation, rising crime, and the lack of everyday essentials.

The government of Venezuela has imposed price controls on many staples, and it's these staples that are in very short supply. Price controls were implemented in response to massive inflation in the country. Venezuela's inflation according to the International Monetary Fund was more than 1,000,000% in 2018.[5]

Inflation results when the money supply expands. Massive hyperinflation, like that being experienced in Venezuela, results when the money supply expands massively.

The government of Venezuela has dramatically expanded the money supply, which has caused significant inflation.

To deal with this debt, the policymakers in Venezuela have the same three choices as many policymakers historically:

Choice one:	Raise taxes
Choice two:	Cut spending
Choice three:	Print money

Predictably, when choice three is a possibility, that's the choice policymakers have usually made throughout history. The policymakers in Venezuela have followed historical precedent, choosing to print money to deal with significant debt. As I previously stated, this option seems the least painful of the three options—at least initially.

But after a while, money printing has consequences, as the citizens of Venezuela are discovering firsthand. Massive inflation is the major consequence of money printing. Money is added to the system far faster than money leaves the system from debt defaults.

Rather than stopping the money printing and cutting spending or raising taxes to deal with the debt, the Venezuelan government decided to take another course of action that is often pursued by policymakers in the same situation. Price controls were implemented to attempt to keep consumer prices low and everyday essentials affordable for the average Venezuelan citizen.

That hasn't worked either; it never does.

Price controls have only kept much-needed everyday staples off store shelves. That's what always happens when price controls are imposed. When manufacturers are forced to sell products at prices below production costs, those manufacturers quit producing and selling those products. That's what is happening in Venezuela and why many essential items are impossible to find.

The average Venezuelan lost twenty-four pounds in 2017 due to a lack of food, skyrocketing inflation, and price controls.[6]

There are only two possible outcomes for Venezuela; they are the same possible outcomes for any country with mammoth debt, including the United States.

The first outcome: You stop the money printing and deal with the debt by raising taxes, cutting spending, or some combination of both. This will result in deflation as the debt is purged from the system. That's what has happened in Greece.

The second outcome: You keep printing money and devaluing your currency until confidence in the currency is lost. After a currency failure and a recalibration of debt to the new currency, deflation sets in as debt is purged from the system. The country of Venezuela is very close to this outcome.

Deflation cannot be avoided by money printing because money printing doesn't make the debt disappear.

Given that context, here are the most important questions:

Does the Federal Reserve begin the money printing again soon?

If the central banks continue to print money, when is confidence lost in these currencies?

If currency printing doesn't begin again in earnest, when does deflation set in?

While I don't know the timing of these events, I do have some great perspective to share with you. The late economist Herbert Stein stated, "If something cannot go on forever, it will stop."

That's profound when you think about it.

Should money printing begin again in earnest, it won't go on forever. It will have to stop at some point; that is something on which we can all agree.

Regardless of when and how, we will see either deflation or inflation followed by deflation. We also know this from studying history.

That being the case, every portfolio should, in my view, contain both an inflation hedge and a deflation hedge.

Before making decisions about the allocation of your portfolio, I believe it's important to thoroughly understand your current investments, what costs are involved, and what the future drawdown potential might be. Sadly, from my experience, many investors have no idea what they are paying in fees to have their investments managed.

Let's begin this discussion with the most basic of investment vehicles and a vehicle that, from my experience, the vast majority of investors own in at least some of their portfolios—mutual funds.

A mutual fund is an investment vehicle that typically owns stocks, bonds, or both.

While there are many ways to categorize mutual funds, I am going to divide them into two general categories: actively managed and passively managed mutual funds.

An actively managed mutual fund has a money manager or team of money managers who decides what securities to buy and sell and when. Some mutual funds own only equities or stocks, while others own only fixed-income vehicles or bonds. There are also balanced funds, which buy both stocks and bonds.

There are also some specialty mutual funds that own other assets, but for the purposes of this discussion, we will focus only on stock funds, bond funds, and balanced funds.

In the case of an actively managed stock fund, the fund manager (or team of fund managers) decides which stocks to buy, which stocks to sell, and when to do so. In the case of an actively managed bond fund, the fund manager (or team of fund managers) decides which fixed-income securities to buy, which fixed-income securities to sell, and when.

A passively managed fund has its investment portfolio mirror the composition of an index. For example, an index fund based on the Standard & Poor's 500 would own the five hundred stocks that make up the Standard & Poor's 500 index. The index fund manager would not make a change in the investment portfolio unless the index changed. Because index funds are more passively managed, fees are typically lower than on funds that are actively managed. Additionally, because turnover is naturally lower in a passively managed index fund than in an actively managed fund, trading costs are also usually lower, and tax consequences are generally more favorable.

While there are exceptions to every rule, passively managed funds based on an index often outperform the majority of actively managed funds with a similar investment objective. A white paper published by Portfolio Solutions and Betterment titled "The Case for Index Fund Portfolios" reviewed portfolios holding ten asset classes between 1997 and 2012. The white paper concluded that index fund portfolios outperformed comparable actively managed portfolios 82% to 90% of the time,[4] largely due to lower taxes and expenses.

While randomly choosing funds is never a good idea, should you decide to engage in a random selection process, your best bet would be to choose index funds over actively managed funds.

There are two kinds of index funds: traditional index mutual funds and exchange-traded funds that are linked to an index. A traditional index mutual fund has its shares priced at the end of each business day, while an index exchange-traded fund trades more like a stock, with the share price fluctuating throughout the day. Both traditional index mutual funds and exchange-traded funds attempt to achieve a return in line with the return achieved by the targeted index.

Many investors are paying higher fees to an actively managed fund and getting returns that are lower than they may have otherwise gotten in a related index fund. While paying higher fees to outperform the return of an index makes good financial sense, paying higher fees to underperform an index makes no financial sense.

In addition to fees paid to mutual fund money managers, as I stated in an earlier chapter, some investors pay a fee to a financial advisor or broker to help the investor choose which funds to own and perhaps when to own them. For example, I have seen many cases in which an investor owns a portfolio of actively managed funds on which the investor may be paying internal management fees of between .5% and 2% per year, and, on top of those fees, the investor was paying a financial advisor or broker another 1% in fees. While there may be instances in which total fees of between 2% and 3% are merited, from my experience, there are far more times when fees of that magnitude are not justified. Always keep in mind that if you are paying total fees of 2% per year, the first 2% you earn each year will end up in the pocket of someone else.

The bottom line here is to completely understand what you are paying in management fees and what you are receiving in return.

When analyzing your current portfolio, there is another very important factor to consider: drawdown. Unfortunately, this factor is rarely discussed.

Drawdown can best be explained as the amount of decline from the high-water mark of an investment to the lowest level of that same investment. For example, assume XYZ stock reached a price of $100 per share at the high-water mark in mid-2007. By March of 2009, let's assume XYZ stock declined to $40 per share. That's a drawdown of 60%.

There is one thing we know about deflation and the stock market from studying history: Stocks don't like deflation. When deflation eventually kicks in, stock prices will decline.

Bond funds don't perform well in an environment of rising interest rates. Given that today's interest rates are at all-time lows and given that the next big move in interest rates is likely to be higher, this could be bad news for bond funds moving ahead.

That's why it's vitally important, in my view, to look at the historical drawdown on the investments you hold in your portfolio. Examine how your investments have performed in bad years in order to give you an idea of what might happen if the worst year were to repeat itself, which I believe is highly likely in the near future, as you read in Chapter Five. I believe that, moving ahead, the outlook for "one bucket" investors is dismal.

The closer you are to needing to use your money, the more important it is to manage drawdown risk. The reason for this is best illustrated. The chart below shows the "break-even curve."

While some investors are familiar with the concept of the "break-even curve," many are not, to their possible detriment.

The break-even curve is simply the percentage gain that's required to completely recoup a loss. Let me explain, using an example.

A 50% loss followed by a 50% gain finds an investor down 25%. For example, if you have $100,000 in an investment account and experience a 50% decline, you'd have $50,000 in the investment account. A subsequent gain of 50% now has the investment account at $75,000.

As the break-even curve in the chart below illustrates, a 100% gain is required after a 50% decline in order to get the investment account back to even.

The larger the decline, the exponentially larger the subse-

Break Even Curve

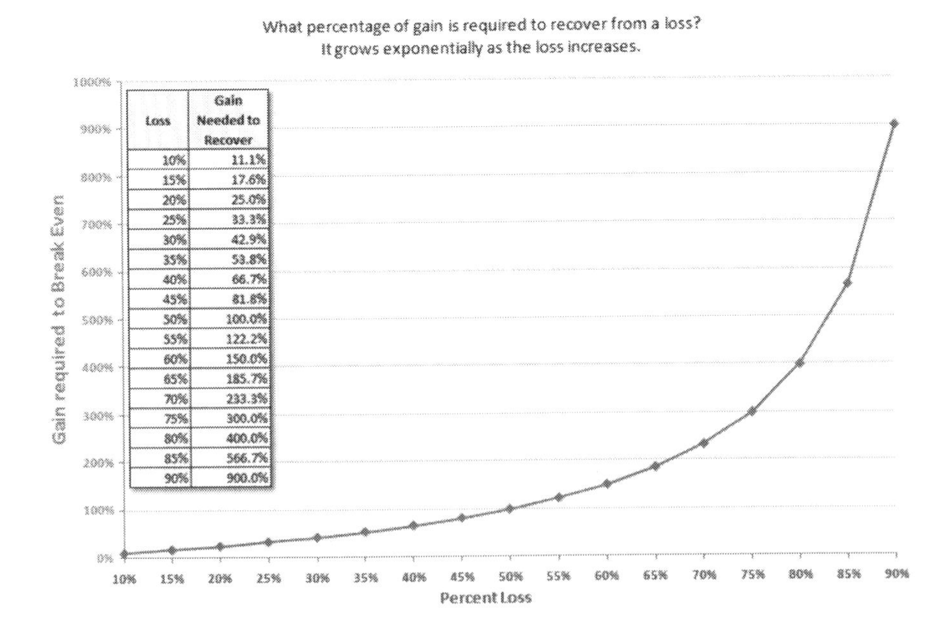

Loss	Gain Needed to Recover
10%	11.1%
15%	17.6%
20%	25.0%
25%	33.3%
30%	42.9%
35%	53.8%
40%	66.7%
45%	81.8%
50%	100.0%
55%	122.2%
60%	150.0%
65%	185.7%
70%	233.3%
75%	300.0%
80%	400.0%
85%	566.7%
90%	900.0%

quent gain has to be to get the account back to even.

A 10% decline requires only an 11.1% gain to get back to even, while a 90% decline, like the Dow Jones Industrial Average experienced during the last economic winter season of the 1930s, requires a 900% gain to get the investment account back to even.

Let me share with you an easy way to conduct this fee and drawdown analysis on your portfolio.

On a piece of paper or a spreadsheet, list the names of your funds or holdings on the left-hand side of the page. Then, next to the name of the fund or holding, list the amount of money you have invested in that holding. Continuing to the right

Fund Stress Test

Fund Name	Value	Total	Existing Fees	ETF Fees	Worst 12 month Return %	Worst 12 Month Return in Dollars
A Fund	$38,577	$38,577	$467	$37	-49.55%	-$19,115
B Fund	$21,508	$21,508	$88	$25	-4.83%	-$1,039
C Fund	$50,134	$50,134	$431	$49	-45.33%	-$22,726
D Fund	$31,750	$31,750	$248	$42	-11.70%	-$3,715
E Fund	$24,732	$24,732	$270	$23	-34.34%	-$8,493
F Fund	$31,753	$31,753	$286	$31	-35.90%	-$11,399
G Fund	$21,087	$21,087	$224	$20	-33.87%	-$7,142
H Fund	$18,772	$18,772	$139	$20	-6.92%	-$1,299
I Fund	$22,642	$22,642	$168	$24	-26.22%	-$5,937
J Fund	$25,487	$25,487	$273	$26	-21.36%	-$5,444
K Fund	$29,649	$29,649	$122	$32	-6.84%	-$2,028
L Fund	$12,760	$12,760	$88	$13	-40.79%	-$5,205
M Fund	$10,678	$10,678	$111	$11	-54.66%	-$5,837
N Fund	$46,134	$46,134	$346	$53	-17.05%	-$7,866
O Fund	$19,471	$19,471	$90	$26	-3.60%	-$701
P Fund	$63,486	$63,486	$489	$63	-43.90%	-$27,870
Q Fund	$39,784	$39,784	$565	$37	-50.96%	-$20,274
	$508,404	Total Fees	$4,402	$531	Total	-$156,089

across the page, list the annual management fee, if there is one, and then just to the right of that, list the percentage loss of the worst twelve months in the fund's history.

You can get this information from the fund's prospectus or by visiting Morningstar's website or using the Thomson Reuters analysis program. Historical drawdown for stocks can be estimated at Yahoo Finance or BigCharts.com.

When your analysis is complete, it might look something like this:

This analysis comes from an actual "Portfolio Stress Test" that my company did for a client. For this example, we have inserted hypothetical fund names in place of the actual fund names.

Notice the existing fees on this portfolio are $4,402 per year. Comparing those fees to the fees this investor might pay on an index exchange-traded fund with a similar investment objective, one sees that the fees in the exchange-traded funds might total only $531 annually. Hypothetically speaking, this investor might save almost $3,900 per year on management fees by moving from actively managed funds to index exchange-traded funds.

For many investors, using actively managed mutual funds for their portfolio may be a bad idea, especially if the portfolio is over $100,000.

Consider the example of the actual Portfolio Stress Test shown above. The investor in this example has a portfolio totaling $508,404 and is paying management fees of $4,402. Another investor who has 10% of the assets of this investor, or a total portfolio of about $50,000, would get the same management as the investor with ten times the assets but would pay only 10% of the fees. The $500,000 investor pays $4,400 annually for management, while the $50,000 investor pays only $440 annually. Yet both investors receive the same exact management job.

The more money you have, the less sense a traditional mutual fund may make for you.

This brings us to drawdown.

The Portfolio Stress Test lists the worst twelve-month returns for these funds historically as a percentage in the second column from the right on the chart. The far-right column shows the actual dollar amount of the decline based on current account balances.

As you can see from the drawdown analysis, this investor might experience a drawdown of $156,089 on a portfolio of $508,404 should the worst year in the market repeat itself. That's a drawdown of more than 30%, which would require nearly a 50% gain after the decline in order to get back to even.

While index exchange-traded funds may reduce fees paid on investments, an investor may still experience drawdown. Exchange-traded funds do nothing to limit drawdown.

That's why I believe exit strategies are imperative, as I stated in the first chapter. Exit strategies may help limit drawdown.

There will be more on this in the next chapter.

[1] Source: *Foreign Policy*, January 9, 2013, "The Greek Depression," by John Sfakianakis, http://www.foreignpolicy.com/articles/2013/01/09/the_greek_depression

[2] Source: http://www.project-syndicate.org/commentary/martin-feldstein-explains-why-reports-of-the-greek-budget-deficit-s-elimination-are-much-exaggerated

[3] Source: http://www.tradingeconomics.com/greece/unemployment-rate

[4] Source: http://www.businessinsider.com/index-funds-beat-actively-managed-funds-2013-6

[5] Source: https://www.reuters.com/article/us-venezuela-economy/imf-projects-venezuela-inflation-will-hit-1000000-percent-in-2018-idUSKBN1KD2L9

[6] Source: https://nationalinterest.org/feature/what-you-should-know-about-socialist-causes-venezuela's-crisis-36612

CHAPTER EIGHT

The "Two Bucket" Approach

By now, you've probably reached the same conclusion as I have. A study of money cycles and economic cycles brings us to the conclusion that we will see deflation; the question is whether we will see inflation or hyperinflation before the deflation kicks in.

In either scenario, using the traditional "one bucket" approach to managing finances will, in my view, lead to certain failure. In an economic winter environment, the traditional asset classes of stocks and bonds used in the "one bucket" approach both decline in value.

In an economic winter environment, using a "two bucket" approach to managing assets will be essential, in my view.

The "two bucket" approach to managing assets has five goals:

1. Reduce fees associated with investments
2. Limit or eliminate investment drawdown during a deflationary environment
3. Hedge for the possibility of inflation or even hyperinflation should the Federal Reserve continue printing
4. Hedge for the possibility of a future fiat currency failure
5. Achieve positive investment returns each year

The "two bucket" approach is a simple, logical way to manage assets. While there is no perfect approach to managing assets, I believe the "two bucket" approach is, by far, the superior method for an economic winter environment such as the one in which we find ourselves today. I developed the "two bucket" approach to managing assets over several years after observing how many of the stockbrokers I supervised gave the traditional "one bucket" advice that miserably failed clients in the 2001 stock market correction.

Year	Return
2000	- 9.11%
2001	-11.89%
2002	-22.10%
2003	+28.68%
2004	+10.88%
2005	+ 4.91%
2006	+15.79%
2007	+ 5.49%
2008	-37.00%
2009	+26.46%
2010	+15.06%
2011	+ 2.11%
2012	+16.00%
2013	+32.39%
2014	+13.48%
2015	+ 1.38%
2016	+11.96%
2017	+21.83%

Again, after the correction of 2008, I saw many clients whose retirement hopes and dreams had been shattered after following the traditional "one bucket" counsel offered by many conventionally trained financial professionals.

To be fair, the "two bucket" approach to managing assets is not without its trade-offs. In a "one bucket" approach, an investor typically has only two primary asset classes in his or her portfolio. This can be good, or it can be bad. The fewer the asset classes in a portfolio, the greater the probability of a terrific year as far as returns are concerned. Because it has fewer asset classes, the "one bucket" approach has the potential to outperform the "two bucket" approach in a great year for stocks. But, in a bad year for stocks, the "one bucket" approach can have an investor experiencing significantly negative returns and even have his or her nest egg devastated. This is when the "one bucket" approach fails.

One need only look at the returns of the S&P 500 of late to understand this point. The data box shows the annual returns of the S&P 500 from calendar year 2000 through calendar year 2017.

The "one bucket" approach comprising stocks and bonds would have seen the stock portion of the portfolio decline by as much as 43.1%, or 37% on a calendar year basis (although actual point-to-point drawdowns during these time frames were much larger). On the other hand, the stock portion of the portfolio would have risen on a calendar year basis by as much as 60.26%, or 92.02%.

Big losses and big returns tend to be typical of the "one bucket" approach to managing money. If the "one bucket" approach to managing assets had a personality, it would have to be described as bipolar. Advocates of the "one bucket" approach point to the big-return years as reasons to use this approach.

Many investors opting for the "one bucket" approach to managing assets are hoping for these big returns but are often taking too much risk for their own individual circumstances. Many of these investors would be better served to seek more consistent, steady returns.

Ask yourself this question: Over a four-year time frame, would you rather have an average annual yield of 25% on your portfolio, or would you prefer a return of 4% per year that is consistent?

Illustration One

$ 100,000 Growing at 4% for 4 years

Beginning Balance: $100,000

Year 1	$104,000
Year 2	$108.160
Year 3	$112,486
Year 4	$116,986

If you answered that question by stating that you'd take the 25% average annual yield, you answered that question exactly as most folks would have. But you answered too hastily.

Let's look at the possibilities.

If you have $100,000 in your investment account and get a 4% return each year for four years, your account balance at the end of the fourth year is illustrated in the box labeled "Illustration One."

Illustration Two

A 25% Average Annual Return

Year 1 Return	- 50%
Year 2 Return	+100%
Year 3 Return	- 50%
Year 4 Return	+100%
Average Annual Return	25%

At the end of the fourth year, assuming a 4% annual return, your $100,000 account has grown to $116,986.

Now let's examine the alternative—a 25% average annual return.

Illustration Two shows just one way to get a 25% average annual return. Notice that a 50% decline followed by a 100% gain followed by a 50% decline followed by a 100% gain results in an average annual return of 25%.

But it also results in a zero total return, as Illustration Three shows.

When your portfolio gets variable or fluctuating returns, the average annual return achieved is far less relevant than the actual net return achieved.

Illustration Three

A 25% Average Annual Return			Balance
Beginning Balance			$100,000
Year 1 Return		- 50%	$ 50,000
Year 2 Return		+100%	$100,000
Year 3 Return		- 50%	$ 50,000
Year 4 Return		+100%	$100,000
Average Annual Return	25%		
Net Return		0%	

"One bucket" advisors often quote average annual returns without discussing *how* the average annual return was arrived at. Unfortunately, that's only half the story. When it comes to discussing average annual returns of an investment vehicle, the question of how a return is achieved is often much more important than the actual return received.

As you can see from this hypothetical example, a 4% consistent return can outperform a 25% average annual return. The "how" is the variable.

Let's go back and look at the annual returns of the S&P 500 from calendar year 2000 through calendar year 2017. The average annual return over that time frame was approximately 7.02%.

Illustration Four

Beginning Balance:		$100,000
Year	Return	Year End Balance
2000	- 9.11%	$ 90,890
2001	-11.89%	$ 80,083
2002	-22.10%	$ 62,385
2003	+28.68%	$ 80,277
2004	+10.88%	$ 89,011
2005	+ 4.91%	$ 93,381
2006	+15.79%	$108,126
2007	+ 5.49%	$114,062
2008	-37.00%	$ 71,859
2009	+26.46%	$ 90,873
2010	+15.06%	$104,458
2011	+ 2.11%	$106,765
2012	+16.00%	$123,847
2013	+32.39%	$163,961
2014	+13.48%	$186,063
2015	+ 1.38%	$188,631
2016	+11.96%	$211,191
2017	+21.83%	$257,294

While an investor can't invest directly in the S&P 500, an investor can invest in a passively managed index fund with the investment objective of duplicating the returns of the S&P 500. For this hypothetical example, let's assume an investor has invested in an index fund that is based on the S&P 500, and let's also assume the fund returns exactly what the S&P 500 index returns.

Illustration Four shows the performance of a $100,000 initial investment based on the returns of the S&P 500. Notice at the end of 2017, the $100,000 had grown to $257,294

Now, contrast that with a 7.02% return every year on a consistent basis. Illustration Five shows that performance. Note how a consistent return of 7.01% annually grows to $339,132, while the average annual return of the S&P 500 grows to only $257,294.

The point?

Given a choice between big potential for gains and consistency, many investors would be better served to seek consistency. This is especially true as one gets closer to needing to use invested assets.

Consistency is one of the five goals of the "two bucket" management system.

The "two bucket" approach to managing assets has a very simple premise. You should divide your assets into two separate buckets of money. Bucket number one is your deflation hedge bucket; it should contain the assets you need to meet your lifestyle needs during retirement. Bucket number two is your inflation hedge bucket; it should contain all your other assets.

Illustration Five

Beginning Balance:		$100,000
Year	Return	Year End Balance
1	+7.02%	$107,020
2	+7.02%	$114,533
3	+7.02%	$122,573
4	+7.02%	$131,178
5	+7.02%	$140,386
6	+7.02%	$150,241
7	+7.02%	$160,788
8	+7.02%	$172,076
9	+7.02%	$184,155
10	+7.02%	$197,083
11	+7.02%	$210,918
12	+7.02%	$225,725
13	+7.02%	$241,571
14	+7.02%	$258,529
15	+7.02%	$276,677
16	+7.02%	$296,101
17	+7.02%	$316,887
18	+7.02%	$339,132

The assets in bucket number one should be invested conservatively with the goal of achieving a predictable, consistent return. This approach will serve an investor well in a deflationary environment. A consistent predictable return with no drawdown will gain purchasing power in a deflationary environment.

The assets in bucket number two should be invested to hedge against inflation, hyperinflation, or a fiat currency failure.

Strict exit strategies should be used when managing "bucket two" assets in order to protect from drawdown.

The assets in bucket number one are paper money assets, which gain purchasing power in a deflationary environment.

When it comes to the assets in bucket number two, however, at least some of the assets should be real, tangible assets that are not the liability of another.

The trouble with the "one bucket" approach advocated by many financial professionals using stocks and bonds or stock mutual funds and bond mutual funds is that all the assets in a portfolio are paper assets. All these assets are usually the liability of another.

This brings me back to the eternal economic truth that no central banker can change, even with massive money printing: If there is too much debt to be paid, not all the debt will be paid.

Since we know there will be defaults on debt, resulting in a deflationary environment, it's important to ask ourselves this question: What assets in my portfolio are the liability of another?

In the case of many portfolios I review, the answer is every asset. That's the nature of paper assets: While these assets are your assets, they are also the liability of another.

When holding paper assets that are the liability of another, we want our counterparty to be as creditworthy as possible.

The reality is that the financial system under which we function uses these paper assets that are the liability of another. So when it comes to selecting the assets in bucket number one, which are the assets you'll use during retirement, we have to use paper assets. We just want to make sure the counterparty on these assets is creditworthy, so we minimize the risk of losing assets.

In a higher yield environment, certificates of deposit (CDs) might be a good choice for some of the assets in bucket number one, provided the bank that issues the CD is creditworthy. Moving ahead in the economic winter season, I do expect to see bank failures, bailouts, and even bail-ins, as we witnessed not long ago in the country of Cyprus. For that reason, I would perform due diligence on the banks with which I did business to ensure these institutions had high safety ratings.

Bucket number one's assets might contain some cash accounts at a bank or credit union. Before making a deposit with a bank or credit union, you want to be sure the institution has high safety ratings. Given that all banks operate under the fractionalized banking system with low reserve requirements, I cannot overstate the importance of understanding the safety of your bank.

In today's artificially low-yield environment, CDs have about the same yield as cash under your mattress, so other than cash needed for current expenses, bank or credit union accounts might not be best to use for "bucket one" assets.

So what asset classes should you consider for the money in bucket number one?

If we go back and look at what asset classes performed best in the last economic winter environment, the 1930s, we find that individual corporate bonds held to maturity were one of the best performing assets of the decade.

Let me be clear: I AM NOT talking about corporate bond mutual funds. Holding a bond mutual fund in an environment of rising interest rates is a surefire way to lose money in bucket number one.

What I am talking about is individual corporate bonds that you plan to hold to maturity.

As we discussed earlier in this book, a bond is a loan to an entity, such as a government or a corporation. While loans to a governmental entity secured by tangible assets, such as a sewer bond or a water bond, might be a reasonable asset to consider for use in bucket number one, for many folks, the higher yields offered by corporate bonds make more sense.

Not all corporate bonds are created equal. Some corporations are far more creditworthy than others. I like to determine how creditworthy a corporation is by looking at its balance sheet and discovering what the corporation owns in tangible assets.

The level of tangible assets owned by a corporation is important for this reason: If you are a bondholder in a company and you've loaned the company money, should that company go out of business for any reason, your loan to the company is collateralized by the assets of the company.

When reviewing a company's balance sheet, two types of assets are listed: real, tangible assets and intangible, paper assets. If a company goes out of business, intangible assets, such as goodwill, won't do you much good.

Let me give you an example.

You buy a bond in a large soft-drink company. Reviewing the company's balance sheet, you discover that it has more than enough tangible assets to pay off its bondholders in the event that it ceases operations. You add this company's bond to your "bucket one" assets.

Now, due to a legislative change, let's assume it is illegal to sell sugary drinks, and the company is forced out of business. You still get all your money because the bond you purchased for your "bucket one" assets was well collateralized with tangible assets. That's one of the best paper assets to own, in my view—one that is fully backed by real, tangible assets.

There are a couple of kinds of corporate bonds I would avoid. Since big banks are still not required to mark their assets to market, which is a valuation process that requires banks to list assets on their balance sheet at their current market value, I would avoid buying bonds in the financial sector. These "mark to market" accounting rules were suspended in the United States and in Europe in 2009 to help avoid more bank failures.

The second type of bond I would avoid adding to "bucket one" assets would be a bond in a highly unionized company. While I have nothing against unions, the now infamous General Motors (GM) bankruptcy that had GM bondholders taking a subservient position to the autoworkers' union is all the proof I need to avoid buying bonds issued by a highly unionized company that could potentially be bailed out by the government. One example of such an industry might be the airline industry.

When deciding how to allocate the assets in bucket number one, you might start by building an income model for your retirement. Figure out how much income you'll need during retirement, determine how much income you'll receive from Social Security, pensions, and other income sources similar to pensions, and then decide how much money you will require from your investments each year. When making this calculation, I would assume a life expectancy of age 95 at a minimum, although many folks are more comfortable planning to age 105.

Illustration Six is an example of how you might lay out this process. Notice how simple the process is. I've only laid out fifteen years for this example, but you'll want to lay out your income model through at least age 95.

Illustration Six

Year	Total Income Needed	Social Security	Pension Income	Needed from "Bucket One" Assets
1	$72,000	$0	$17,000	$55,000
2	$72,000	$0	$17,000	$55,000
3	$72,000	$25,000	$17,000	$30,000
4	$72,000	$25,000	$17,000	$30,000
5	$72,000	$36,000	$17,000	$19,000
6	$72,000	$36,000	$17,000	$19,000
7	$72,000	$36,000	$17,000	$19,000
8	$72,000	$36,000	$17,000	$19,000
9	$72,000	$36,000	$17,000	$19,000
10	$72,000	$36,000	$17,000	$19,000
11	$72,000	$36,000	$17,000	$19,000
12	$72,000	$36,000	$17,000	$19,000
13	$72,000	$36,000	$17,000	$19,000
14	$72,000	$36,000	$17,000	$19,000
15	$72,000	$36,000	$17,000	$19,000

The income model example in Illustration Six assumes this hypothetical couple is retiring before they are electing to collect their Social Security benefits. That means they will need to depend on more income from their investments during the first few years of retirement and then less on their investments during later years. For many retirees, waiting to collect Social Security benefits or collecting a "free" spousal benefit while a primary benefit continues to grow can be a great strategy.

An entire book could be written on different ways to maximize Social Security benefits; in fact, I've written one, and such a discussion would go well beyond the scope of this book. If you have not yet determined how to collect your Social Security benefits, there are a number of good resources to help you understand your options including my book, *The Little Black Book on Maximizing Social Security Benefits*.

Illustration Six has this hypothetical retired couple needing to draw $55,000 per year from their investment assets during the first two years of retirement, $30,000 per year during years three and four of retirement, and then $19,000 per year thereafter.

Since this is income this couple will require to meet their retirement lifestyle desires, the assets needed to produce this income are "bucket one" assets. Since income of $55,000 will be needed during the first year of retirement, that money should probably just be set aside in a money market account.

Another $55,000 is needed during the second year of retirement, so we might have this couple go out and buy a bond maturing in one year. Depending on the bond yield, we would "back into" the deposit amount needed to have $55,000 in one year. Assuming a hypothetical 2% return, a deposit of $53,922 might be needed to provide $55,000 in one year.

Since $30,000 is required to meet income needs during the third year of retirement, we would again potentially "back into" a required investment amount in order to produce $30,000 to use to meet income needs in year three of retirement.

You get the idea.

We would continue building a laddered bond portfolio of highly rated individual corporate bonds with maturities matching up with when the money will be needed for retirement income.

This is a great exercise in which to engage when you are trying to determine when you might be able to retire or if you are able to retire at all. It will help you determine what level of assets you might need to meet your income desires during retirement.

If you don't know how much income you might need during retirement, don't feel bad; you're not alone. From my experience, many people don't know this number without doing some research. One of the best ways to do this research is to track your past expenses. Just go back and log your expenses for one year, and you'll have a pretty good idea of what you might need for income during retirement.

From my experience, the old rule of thumb that says you'll need only a portion of your working income during retirement isn't true for most folks. Unless you're getting rid of a car, downsizing a house, or planning some other major lifestyle change during retirement, your income needs during retirement might not change all that much.

Using laddered maturity corporate bond assets for bucket one can be an effective and efficient way to meet your income needs during retirement. There is another advantage to using laddered maturity corporate bonds for "bucket one" assets. When you do this and hold the bonds to maturity, you are not exposing yourself to the same drawdown risk as you would when using a bond mutual fund as long as you choose your bonds wisely. And there is no ongoing management fee being deducted.

There is another alternative for "bucket one" assets: It's also a corporate bond-based strategy when utilized properly.

Rather than purchase a portfolio of highly rated corporate bonds with laddered maturity dates, you might also consider making a deposit into an annuity account with a highly rated insurance company that invests its assets in corporate bonds.

But be careful: Not all annuities are created equal. Some annuity accounts require you to leave money on deposit for a minimum time frame, while others require you to take an income from them, forfeiting access to your lump sum. Many of these annuity contracts should be avoided, in my opinion.

Variable annuity contracts offer the option to have your purchase payment invested in a market-related subaccount. These accounts are often expensive and may put assets needed for income at risk in the stock market. For the purposes of "bucket one" assets, I believe investors should avoid these types of annuities as well.

On the other hand, there are annuity accounts that are term specific. You can purchase an annuity for a one-year period, a two-year period, a three-year period, or almost any other time-specific period.

Using time period–specific annuities, you can structure a portfolio of annuities with laddered maturity dates in much the same way as you would build a portfolio of laddered maturity corporate bonds. Once you have your income model constructed, you once again "back into" the amount you'll need to deposit in order to produce the income you want when you want it.

Insurance companies operate under a set of reserving rules that differ completely from those of banks. As we already discussed, banks are required to reserve 10% of deposited assets in the fractionalized banking system. Insurance companies, on the other hand, are required to reserve 100% of the assets the company might need to disperse in benefit payments.

Time period–specific annuities can also offer another advantage: You are more likely to be able to purchase an annuity for the exact amount you'll need. In the case of laddered maturity corporate bonds, one may have to buy a slightly larger quantity than is actually needed to meet income needs since bonds are issued in $1,000 increments. For this reason, time period–specific annuities may make sense for "bucket one" assets for many people planning for their retirement income.

Always remember to do your due diligence before purchasing corporate bonds or time period–specific annuities. In the case of corporate bonds, make certain you thoroughly understand what tangible assets the company holds, and in the case of time period–specific annuities, ensure that the insurance company with which you are dealing is sound and owns bonds that are collateralized by tangible assets.

Remember, we want "bucket one" assets to perform as predictably as possible. In a deflationary environment, these "bucket one" assets will gain buying power as income is paid out.

"Bucket two" assets are your assets to protect you from inflation, hyperinflation, or a fiat currency failure.

You probably noticed that when I presented the hypothetical income model to you, I didn't adjust the income needed annually for inflation. There are three reasons for this.

One, from my experience, many clients don't need an inflation adjustment on their income during retirement. While there are exceptions, it's been my experience that people spend less during retirement as they get older. While there may be lots of travel and other "bucket list" activities in which people engage during the early years of their retirement, these activities generally wane as time passes.

Two, assuming deflation kicks in sooner rather than later, the income coming from bucket one will gain purchasing power.

Three, if inflation adjustments are needed at a future date, this additional income should come from "bucket two" assets, which will be invested to provide an inflation hedge.

So, how should "bucket two" assets be allocated?

The primary goal of bucket number two is to provide an inflation hedge should the policy response of the central bank be to continue to print money. Massive money printing will, at some point, cause inflation, especially if money starts moving more quickly through the fractionalized banking system.

Historically speaking, two of the best inflation hedges have been gold and silver; however, there are many different possible ways to own gold and silver. So what kind of gold or silver should you buy?

For starters, if possible, avoid paper assets whose price action is correlated to gold or silver. Many exchange-traded funds do a reasonably good job of tracking the price of gold and silver but don't guarantee the fund will actually own the metal.

For that reason, I often recommend that investors avoid exchange-traded funds and buy the real metal, provided they can store it safely.

When it comes to silver, a good choice for many folks would be pre-1965 US quarters, half dollars, or dimes. These coins minted prior to 1965 contained real silver, unlike the coins that are minted today. A pre-1965 US quarter has a silver content of .18084 troy ounces. This means that if the price of silver is $15 per ounce, the silver value of one quarter would be about $2.71. A pre-1965 US half dollar has silver content of .36169 troy ounces (twice the silver content of a pre-1965 US quarter). Assuming the same price of silver of $15 per ounce, the value of just one of these pre-1965 US half dollars would be about $5.42. A pre-1965 US dime has silver content of 40% of a quarter and 20% of a half dollar.

There are many places to buy these coins, which are known as "junk silver." When purchasing, be sure to calculate the price being asked for the coin in relation to the coin's actual silver content. For example, if the spot price (the current market ask price) of silver is $15 per ounce, the silver value of one pre-1965 US quarter would be calculated as follows:

$$\$15 \times .18084 = \$2.71$$

You will not be able to find a place to buy these coins for the spot price of silver. There are many reputable dealers who sell these coins, and I would estimate that you could expect to pay from 10% to 15% over the spot price of silver, unless the coins that you were buying had collector value in addition to the intrinsic value of the silver contained in the coin.

If you want to buy gold in addition to silver, you could consider pre-1933 US coins.

From 1907 through 1933, the United States minted a $20 St. Gaudens gold piece that contained about one ounce of gold. If you buy the coins in MS-63 or MS-64 condition, you may find that they trade for a premium ranging from 15% to 30% over the spot price of gold.

I like owning silver and gold in US currency to hedge against another 1933-style gold bullion confiscation. In the 1933 order that required all Americans to turn in their gold bullion, there was an exception made for collector coins or coins that could have numismatic value.

Not only do the gold and silver holdings I've recommended have potential numismatic value, but they are also still technically US currency.

If you are using retirement account assets to purchase gold, you'll need to use an approved gold bullion coin like an American Eagle or a Canadian Maple Leaf and arrange to store your coins in a secure storage facility and ensure that the required IRS annual reporting is done as well.

So how much gold and silver should you buy?

I like weighting metals holdings toward gold. It's far easier to store a lot of value in gold than in silver. For many folks, once you've determined how much of your "bucket two" assets should be in tangible metals, a ratio of 80% to 90% gold to 10% to 20% silver might be advisable.

The percentage of your overall portfolio that should be invested in precious metals will vary by person and individual circumstances. If you're already retired and you have limited assets, requiring you to have more of your overall portfolio in bucket one, you may have fewer assets, such as precious metals, available for investment in bucket two.

In an ideal world, arbitrarily speaking, you might have a minimum of 10% of your overall portfolio in precious metals.

While precious metals have performed well historically in an inflationary environment, they have also often done well in a deflationary environment. As we have discussed, deflation is inevitable given current private sector debt levels.

While it was illegal to own gold in the last economic winter season of the 1930s, making it difficult to know what the actual market price of the metals was, it is possible to extrapolate the performance of gold during the 1930s by observing how gold stocks performed.

The mining company Homestake Mining was a leading, publicly traded mining company when the economic winter season of the 1930s hit. In May of 1924, during the economic autumn season, shares in Homestake Mining sold for $39. At that time, the Dow Jones Industrial Average stood at 90.

By the market peak in August of 1929, a little more than five years later, the Dow Jones Industrial Average had more than quadrupled, reaching the 380 level. While Homestake Mining stock also rose to about $90 per share during that time frame, the Dow's gains almost doubled the gains of Homestake Mining's stock on a percentage basis.

However, when deflation appeared, the story changed. Stocks don't like deflation. The Dow Jones Industrial Average fell to 42 by the time the stock market bottomed, resulting in a decline of about 90%. During that same time frame, Homestake Mining's share price rose to 528 by 1939 for a gain of 486%.

Given that we are confident, from our study of history, that we will see inflation or inflation followed by deflation, precious metals are an essential portion of our "bucket two" assets.

From my research, there is one other viable inflation hedge that also incorporates gold. This strategy was first developed in the 1970s during the last economic summer season. Financial radio host and author Harry Browne wrote about this strategy in his newsletter in the 1970s and then later in his book *Why the Best-Laid Investment Plans Usually Go Wrong*, published in 1987.

Browne developed this approach to money management with the objectives of achieving positive investment returns each year (also known as an absolute returns investment strategy) and keeping pace with inflation. While there is no guarantee that the objective will be achieved, historically speaking, it has demonstrated itself to be an effective strategy.

Browne dubbed the strategy the "permanent portfolio." Browne designed the portfolio to withstand almost any circumstance, whether a banking crisis, a sovereign debt crisis, a stock market crash, or a deflationary collapse. It's interesting that even though Browne developed this strategy more than forty years ago, each of these circumstances exists somewhere in the world today.

Browne concluded, as I have from my research, that in order to be able to weather any of these circumstances, the portfolio needs to be diversified in more than the two traditional asset classes of stocks and bonds. Using different terminology than I do, Browne advocated against the traditional "one bucket" approach promoted by the financial industry.

In the permanent portfolio, Browne advocated holding four different asset classes, each of which would respond predictably to a particular economic condition:

1. **Common stocks:** This category will likely produce profits in periods of general prosperity.
2. **Gold:** This asset will likely produce profits during periods of rising inflation or currency crisis and perform well in a deflationary environment.
3. **Bonds:** This asset will produce a profit during periods of falling interest rates, such as when inflation is declining and in the latter stages of deflation.

4. **Cash:** This asset provides stability when no investments are doing well and provides purchasing power gains in a deflationary environment.

Browne's permanent portfolio approach makes sense given that we've already established that stocks have historically done well in two of the four economic seasons, and gold has performed well in the other two economic seasons.

Assembling Browne's permanent portfolio is easy.

Twenty-five percent of the amount invested should be in common stocks using a total stock market exchange-traded fund. These funds are very inexpensive to hold and provide returns that are approximately commensurate with the stock market.

Twenty-five percent of the invested total can be in gold. A word of caution here: As I've already discussed, I would not use a gold exchange-traded fund; instead, I would suggest opting for the real metal. If you choose to use the real metal, I would advise buying the metal and taking delivery of it or using a company that will store your physical gold for you in a secure vault outside the banking system. In addition, make sure that it's an allocated gold holding where your gold is actually segregated from the gold of other investors. You don't want to own a share of a 400-ounce bar. You want to be able to have the gold shipped to you if you desire.

Twenty-five percent of the invested total should be in long-term US Treasury bills. While I am not optimistic about the long-term outlook for US Treasuries, at present, they are the best of a bunch of bad choices when it comes to providing a safe haven for investors.

Twenty-five percent of the invested total should be in cash. You can use US Treasury bills or a money market at a highly rated financial institution.

On an annual basis, your permanent portfolio allocations get rebalanced to 25% in each of the four asset classes.

For example's sake, let's look at calendar year 2017. If, at the beginning of 2017, you had invested $20,000 in a permanent portfolio, with 25% or $5,000 allocated to each of the four asset classes as outlined above, at the end of 2017, your new portfolio balance might look approximately like this:

Growth stocks	$ 5,971
US bonds	$ 5,125
Gold	$ 5,641
Cash	$ 5,050
New balance	$21,787

At year end, you would rebalance to a 25% allocation in each asset class. Since 25% of $21,787 is $5,446.75, that's the total that should be invested in each asset class for the next year. The allocation doesn't have to be exact—just fairly close.

This is an easy way to manage your assets, it requires little time, and you don't have to pay anyone to manage anything. This can be an especially attractive option for someone to consider if he or she is currently paying ongoing fees based on a percentage of assets being managed, depending on their investment objectives. Historically speaking, this approach has been very effective.

My company has developed what we believe is a more efficient way to utilize Browne's permanent portfolio strategy. Based upon our proprietary analysis of each of these markets, we may be overweight in certain asset classes. Our modeling of these derivations of Browne's strategy can show better results than Browne's once-per-year rebalancing.

Depending on the level of assets you have in bucket two, you might also consider a third strategy—a strategy I call the managed risk strategy.

The objectives of the managed risk strategy are to preserve assets and achieve a 1% to 10% growth rate each year and not lose money. (There is no guarantee that the objective will be achieved.)

The managed risk strategy can best be explained through the use of a hypothetical example.

Jack has $65,000 invested in an index fund that we'll call XYZ fund. He owns five hundred shares of XYZ fund at a share price of $130. XYZ fund is passively managed to attempt to achieve the same approximate performance as a market index.

Should the related market index decline by 50%, Jack would likely find that his investment would decline by about 50%. On the other hand, if the related index were to appreciate by 50%, Jack would find that his investment would also appreciate by approximately 50%. When Jack has some of his assets invested in an index fund, theoretically speaking, 100% of his assets are at risk. As we've established, in an economic winter environment, this could be risky.

Rather than risk 100% (theoretically) of his capital in XYZ fund, Jack decides to take his $65,000 and go purchase individual corporate bonds. As we have already established, it's important to note that Jack **does not** buy bond funds. The corporate bonds that Jack buys are from the secondary market and have laddered maturity dates. Since we have already discussed the desired criterion for buying bonds, I won't repeat them here.

Jack decides which bonds he will buy and diversifies his holdings, buying no more than five bonds in any one company. Since bonds are typically denominated in increments of $1,000, Jack owns bonds issued by twelve different companies, which further reduces his risk through diversification. In this hypothetical example, let's assume that Jack realizes an average yield to maturity on his bond portfolio of 4%.

This means that Jack will earn interest of $2,600 annually on his portfolio of $65,000.

Jack likes the safety of his portfolio since he's now insulated himself from a stock market crash; however, Jack would like to have the opportunity to get returns that are greater than the 4% interest that he is earning on his bond portfolio.

Jack should consider combining this strategy of buying highly rated corporate bonds with a strategy that uses some of the interest he earns on his corporate bonds to buy call options on the exchange-traded index fund that he owned.

When it comes to buying options, the only thing that many investors have heard is that options are risky—maybe even very risky. While this can be true, it isn't always true. If you were to sell options to an investor, collecting money for the sale, your risk could be significant. If you buy an option, your maximum risk is the amount of money that you paid for the option.

I can best explain options by using a real estate analogy with which you may be familiar. Let's say that there is a piece of property that you really want to own, but the owner doesn't want to sell it. You might consider offering to buy an option on the property from the property owner. You would give the owner of the property some money, and in exchange, the owner would grant you the first right of refusal to buy the property should the owner ever decide to sell it. Should the owner ever decide to sell the property, you would have the option to buy the property, but you wouldn't be obligated to make the purchase.

Call options on an exchange-traded index fund (or stock) work in a similar manner. You part with some money, and in exchange, you receive an option to buy a specified number of shares of an exchange-traded fund at a predetermined price, provided you do so prior to an expiration date. To summarize, there are three components when buying a call option:

1. The predetermined price at which the security can be purchased, which is also known as the "strike price."

2. The number of shares: The cost to buy an option on one share is multiplied by the number of shares on which you would like an option to purchase. Options are purchased in contracts of one hundred shares each.

3. The expiration date: The longer it is until the option expires, the more expensive the option typically is.

Going back to our example, let's assume that Jack wants to buy some call options on XYZ fund. Since the current share price is $130 per share, Jack decides that his strike price (predetermined purchase price) will be $130 per share. Jack discovers that he can buy a call option on one share of XYZ fund, expiring in six months, for $5.60 per share, or he could buy a call option with the same strike price of $130 per share with an expiration date of twelve months for $8.10 per share. Since one option contract allows the buyer to control one hundred shares, one contract with a $130 strike price expiring in six months will cost Jack $560 ($5.60 per share x 100 shares), or one contract with a $130 strike price expiring in twelve months will cost Jack $810 ($8.10 per share x 100 shares).[8]

While both contracts will allow Jack to purchase one hundred shares of XYZ fund at a price of $130 per share, one contract expires in about six months, while the other contract expires in about twelve months. The contract that expires in twelve months costs more per share than the contract expiring in six months, even though all the other terms of the contract are exactly the same. This demonstrates that the cost of an option is made up of two components—the strike price (predetermined purchase price) and the time until the option expires. The closer the current price to the strike price, the more expensive the option contract will be. For example, if XYZ fund is being sold for $130 per share, it would be cheaper to buy a $131 strike price option than a $130 strike price option since the price of the underlying security needs to move further to hit the $131 strike price. The time factor of the cost of an option contract is just common sense; it is cheaper to buy an option that expires in six months than it is to buy an option that expires in one year, since the one-year option gives the option buyer twice as much time for the share price to rise to a desired level.

In Jack's case, let's assume that he decides that he is willing to risk up to half the interest that he will earn on his corporate bonds to buy call options on XYZ fund. Since Jack will earn $2,600 in interest on the corporate bonds, he is willing to risk up to $1,300 to buy options.

Assuming Jack buys call option contracts that have a six-month expiration date, Jack can buy two option contracts at a cost of $560 each for a total of $1,120 and control two hundred shares of XYZ fund. Now, any time within the next six months, Jack can exercise his option and buy two hundred shares of XYZ fund for $130 per share.

There are only two possible outcomes for Jack, and provided the corporate bonds perform as anticipated, Jack makes money on both outcomes.

In the first outcome, the call options that Jack purchased will be exercised. If we were to assume that XYZ fund went to $160 per share prior to the expiration date and Jack exercised the options, Jack would be able to buy two hundred shares of XYZ fund for $130 per share and simultaneously sell the shares for $160 for a profit of $6,000. When the $6,000 profit from exercising the options is added to the corporate bond interest that Jack elected to keep totaling $1,480, a gain of $7,480 would be realized. This translates to a gain of about 12% and a total year-end account balance of $72,480.

The second outcome has XYZ fund's share price falling in value. Assuming XYZ fund's share price declined to $100 per share, Jack wouldn't exercise his options. After all, why would someone exercise an option to buy two hundred shares of a fund for $130 per share when the current share price is $100? Assuming the share price of XYZ fund declined and Jack did not exercise his options, Jack would still keep the remaining interest of $1,480 and forfeit the cost of the option. Jack's year-end balance would still be $66,480 in this example.

The first potential outcome in this hypothetical example is an admittedly good outcome. The second possible outcome is a worst-case scenario outcome, provided the corporate bonds perform as expected. Looks pretty good, doesn't it? You potentially make money with option two or make more money with option one. So, what is the downside?

The downside to this strategy is that an investor trades off growth potential for possible principle protection. Should XYZ fund go to $160 per share by continuing to hold the shares of XYZ fund and risk his or her capital, an investor would see his or her investment rise to a value of $80,000 rather than the $72,480 that the investor made in this example. Put another way, in an up market, taking risk with one's principle would provide a larger profit at year end.

On the other hand, should XYZ fund decline, the year-end account balance remains positive if the corporate bonds perform as anticipated rather than decline to $50,000, assuming a share price of $100.

For many investors, this is a reasonable trade-off since we have already discussed the break-even curve and the difference between average annual returns and consistent returns.

So there you have it: The "two bucket" approach is one that I believe will be critical to not only surviving but prospering through the rest of this economic winter season.

CHAPTER NINE

Implementing the "Two Bucket" Approach in Your Situation

How you implement the "two bucket" approach in your situation is dependent on your own individual facts and circumstances.

If you are more than ten to fifteen years away from retirement, you might consider putting an approximately equal amount of assets in bucket one, the deflation hedge bucket, and in bucket two, the inflation hedge bucket.

If you are more than ten to fifteen years away from retirement, the goal is to position your assets to give you the best opportunity to get consistent, steady returns and avoid big drawdowns that require huge gains to get back to your investment's prior high.

If you are closer to retirement and have more immediate or greater income needs, you may want to weight assets more to the first bucket or the deflation hedge bucket. The lower the level of income you will need from your investments, the fewer the assets you will place in bucket one, leaving more assets for bucket two.

As we've discussed, the best way to get started is to do a Portfolio Stress Test on your existing portfolio. Learn exactly what your current costs are as far as money management fees are concerned and what the historic drawdown has been on your existing holdings.

If you are over age 55, you'd also be wise to begin to understand what your Social Security collection options are so that you can incorporate them into your income model once you've identified your desired income level during retirement. You'll also want to incorporate any other income to which you may be entitled during retirement, such as pension income or rental income.

Once you've built your income model and understand how much income you'll get and from what sources, you can "plug in" the level of income you'll need from your investments. Once you know how much income you'll need from your investments, you can then calculate the level of assets you'll need in buckets one and two.

Let me give you an example[1] of how to follow this process. It's a similar process to the one our New Retirement Rules™ advisors follow with clients when helping them develop their own money management plan to help them potentially:

1. Reduce fees associated with investments. (Often the net cost of doing a plan with one of our New Retirement Rules™ advisors is zero or even creates positive cash flow due to savings on fees and taxes.)

2. Limit or eliminate investment drawdown during a deflationary environment.

3. Hedge for the possibility of inflation or even hyperinflation should the Federal Reserve resume currency printing in earnest.

4. Hedge for the possibility of a future fiat currency failure.
5. Achieve positive investment returns each year.

In this hypothetical example, we'll look at the case of Bill and Sarah. Bill and Sarah are both 66 years old. Sarah will retire immediately, while Bill will work for another two years. Both Bill and Sarah have worked through the years; however, Bill has earned slightly more than Sarah has earned on average.

Bill and Sarah own their home free and clear and also own a cottage free and clear.

They have a nonqualified (non-IRA or nonretirement account) brokerage account in which they own mutual funds consisting of stocks and bonds. The current market value of the holdings in this account is $235,000.

Bill has 401(k) assets of $437,000 and IRA assets of $67,000. Sarah has IRA assets of $124,000.

Bill and Sarah expect to need $72,000 per year in retirement income to meet their lifestyle desires.

Bill will work until age 70 since he loves what he does. Sarah will retire at her Normal Retirement Age of 66 and 2 months.

When Bill reaches the age of 70, he will begin to collect his primary Social Security benefit of $38,014 annually. When added to Sarah's benefit of $27,047, their total household Social Security benefit will be $65,061 annually.

Since Bill and Sarah are both in good health, they elect to maximize their Social Security benefits in this manner.

Bill and Sarah desire $84,000 annually in retirement income and will need that income to begin when Bill retires at his age

70. Since Bill and Sarah have elected to defer collecting their primary Social Security benefits until age 70, they will need to rely more heavily on their investments for income during the first two years of retirement and then rely less on their investments once they both reach age 70 and have begun to collect their primary Social Security benefit amounts.

Bill and Sarah's income model looks like this:

Bill and Sarah's Income Model

Year	Total Income Needed	Social Security	Pension Income	Needed from "Bucket One" Assets
1	$0 (Bill employed)	$0	$0	$0
2	$0 (Bill employed)	$0	$0	$0
3	$84,000	$65.061	$0	$18,939
4	$84,000	$65,061	$0	$18,939
5	$84,000	$65,061	$0	$18,939
6	$84,000	$65,061	$0	$18,939
7	$84,000	$65,061	$0	$18,939
8	$84,000	$65,061	$0	$18,939
9	$84,000	$65,061	$0	$18,939
10	$84,000	$65,061	$0	$18,939
11	$84,000	$65,061	$0	$18,939
12	$84,000	$65,061	$0	$18,939
13	$84,000	$65,061	$0	$18,939
14	$84,000	$65,061	$0	$18,939
15	$84,000	$65,061	$0	$18,939

Again, I've run the income model for fifteen years, which would be until Bill and Sarah turn 81. It would be advisable to run Bill and Sarah's income model through a minimum of age 95, perhaps even age 105.

Given what Bill and Sarah will need for income during retirement, and given their investable assets of $863,000, we now need to help Bill and Sarah determine how many assets to allocate to bucket number one, which is the deflation bucket, and bucket number two, which is the inflation bucket.

Assuming Bill and Sarah live to age 105, the assets that need to be allocated to bucket one, or the deflation bucket, are $390,000. These assets will be deposited in a combination of highly rated corporate bonds and time period–specific annuities. In Bill and Sarah's income plan design, this level of assets in bucket number one will be enough to provide them with their desired level of income through their age of 105.

Remember that bucket number one is the deflation bucket. If deflation kicks in sooner rather than later, the buying power of the assets in bucket number one will increase.

Since Bill and Sarah have total invested assets of $863,000, and $390,000 will be deposited in bucket number one, that leaves $473,000 to be deposited in bucket number two. Bucket number two is the inflation hedge bucket. The assets in this bucket will be invested in inflation hedges. As we discussed in the previous chapter, these assets might be invested in a combination of precious metals, the permanent portfolio or a variation thereof, and the managed risk strategy. These assets have performed well historically in an inflationary environment and have not suffered from significant drawdowns in a deflationary environment. This may make them good allocation choices in this economic winter climate.

Another aspect of developing an effective plan that goes beyond the scope of this book is to determine the tax character of the assets in each bucket. By tax character, I'm referring to whether the assets in each bucket are 401(k) or IRA assets, Roth IRA assets, or nonqualified assets (assets on which income taxes have already been paid).

When developing some income plans, in addition to identifying fee savings and putting protection in place from potential drawdowns, it is often possible to also find tax savings on retirement accounts.

When projecting the level of taxes that one might pay on retirement account assets during one's lifetime with no IRA tax management plan and then comparing that number to the level of taxes one might pay if an IRA tax management program were implemented, significant savings can often be realized. Additional, temporary tax savings opportunities on retirement accounts may exist for many IRA and 401(k) owners under the recently passed tax legislation.

I've discovered that many IRA investors don't have a clear picture of the tax ramifications of owning IRA assets.

There is one fact that's critically important to remember when it comes to understanding the ultimate tax consequences of retirement accounts: They are joint accounts you have with the IRS. When it comes to the taxes you'll pay on your retirement account, it's not a question of if you'll pay the income taxes due; it's a question of when.

You can allow retirement account assets to accumulate and avoid tax on withdrawals until you reach age 70½, but, at that point, you will be required to begin to make distributions from your retirement account based on a required minimum distribution schedule published by the IRS. These distributions are taxable at ordinary income tax rates on your tax return.

The IRA Analysis table that follows illustrates[2] the total taxes a 66-year-old IRA investor might pay on an IRA account, assuming a 25% combined income tax rate, a 4% annual return, and life expectancy to age 95.

Notice from the IRA Analysis table that total taxes paid on a $500,000 IRA account based on these assumptions is $273,869. That's an effective tax rate of 55% of present IRA value!

I should point out that if growth rates are lower than 4%, taxes paid will be less; but if growth rates are greater than 4%, taxes will be higher.

There is one additional variable to consider: future income tax rates. If future income tax rates are higher than current income tax rates, the ultimate tax paid on your retirement accounts could increase as well. Under current tax law, personal income tax rates revert back to the old, higher rates after eight years.

To be fair, if tax rates decline, total income tax paid could be lower than illustrated in the IRA Analysis table.

When putting together an income and allocation plan, the tax character of the assets in each bucket should be carefully considered in order to maximize tax savings in addition to working toward these five goals:

1. Reduce fees associated with investments
2. Limit or eliminate investment drawdown during a deflationary environment
3. Hedge for the possibility of inflation or even hyperinflation should the Federal Reserve continue printing currency
4. Hedge for the possibility of a future fiat currency failure
5. Achieve positive investment returns each year

IRA Analysis

Client: Sample Client

Assumption:

Assumed Growth Rate:	4%
Assumed Combined Tax Rate:	25%
Current IRA Balance:	$500,000
Client Age:	66
Waithdrawls:	RMD's Only

Year	Age	Balance	RMD Factor	Income Withdrawl (RMD Amount)
1	66	$500,000	$0	$0
2	67	$520,000	$0	$0
3	68	$540,800	$0	$0
4	69	$562,432	$0	$0
5	70	$584,929	$27	$21,348
6	71	$586,125	$27	$22,118
7	72	$586,567	$26	$22,913
8	73	$586,201	$25	$23,733
9	74	$584,966	$24	$24,578
10	75	$582,804	$23	$25,450
11	76	$579,648	$22	$26,348
12	77	$575,432	$21	$27,143
13	78	$570,221	$20	$28,090
14	79	$563,816	$20	$28,914
15	80	$556,299	$19	$29,749
16	81	$547,612	$18	$30,593
17	82	$537,700	$17	$31,444
18	83	$526,506	$16	$32,301
19	84	$513,973	$16	$33,160
20	85	$500,046	$15	$33,787
21	86	$484,909	$14	$34,391
22	87	$468,539	$13	$34,966
23	88	$450,917	$13	$35,505
24	89	$432,028	$12	$36,002
25	90	$411,867	$11	$36,129
26	91	$390,768	$11	$36,182
27	92	$368,769	$10	$36,154
28	93	$345,920	$10	$36,033
29	94	$322,282	$9	$35,416
30	95	$298,341	$9	$34,691

IRA Analysis

Taxes on Income and RMD's	Cumulative Tax	Net to Heirs	Net to Spouse
$0	$0	$375,000	$500,000
$0	$0	$390,000	$520,000
$0	$0	$405,600	$540,800
$0	$0	$421,824	$562,432
$5,337	$5,337	$438,697	$584,929
$5,529	$10,866	$439,594	$586,125
$5,728	$16,594	$439,925	$586,567
$5,933	$22,527	$439,650	$586,201
$6,145	$28,672	$438,725	$584,966
$6,362	$35,034	$437,103	$582,804
$6,587	$41,621	$434,736	$579,648
$6,786	$48,407	$431,574	$575,432
$7,022	$55,429	$427,665	$570,221
$7,228	$62,657	$422,862	$563,816
$7,437	$70,094	$417,224	$556,299
$7,648	$77,742	$410,709	$547,612
$7,861	$85,603	$403,275	$537,700
$8,075	$93,678	$394,879	$526,506
$8,290	$101,968	$385,480	$513,973
$8,447	$110,415	$375,034	$500,046
$8,598	$119,013	$363,682	$484,909
$8,741	$127,754	$351,405	$468,539
$8,876	$136,630	$338,188	$450,917
$9,001	$145,631	$324,021	$432,028
$9,032	$154,663	$308,900	$411,867
$9,046	$163,709	$293,076	$390,768
$9,038	$172,747	$276,577	$368,769
$9,008	$181,755	$259,440	$345,920
$8,854	$190,609	$241,711	$322,282
$8,673	$199,282	$223,756	$298,341
Additonal Tax at Death:		**$74,585**	
	Total Tax:	**$273,869**	

Additional Resources

To help you not only protect yourself in this economic winter environment but also potentially prosper, I have made some additional resources available.

You may visit www.YourPortfolioWatch.com to sign up for my weekly "Portfolio Watch" newsletter. This publication is free and delivered via e-mail. Rest assured, we never share or sell your e-mail information.

If you have investable assets of $250,000 or more, you may qualify to receive a free Portfolio Stress Test that will do the following:

- Provide you with a Social Security maximization analysis
- Identify the current fees you are paying in your portfolio
- Identify historical drawdown in your portfolio
- Provide you with an IRA Tax Analysis

This Portfolio Stress Test is provided free of charge.

In order to prepare a customized Portfolio Stress Test for you, we need to get some information from you. We NEVER ask for personal information, such as account numbers or Social Security numbers, and you should never provide them to anyone.

We only need a few bits of information that will be readily available to you in order to prepare your Portfolio Stress Test. Once completed, we will forward your Portfolio Stress Test to you for your review.

It will be a valuable tool in helping you develop your "two

bucket" approach to managing finances in the current economic winter environment.

You may be wondering why we do a free Portfolio Stress Test. Simple: It's a great way for you to get some value and another perspective and a good way for us to introduce folks to the work we do.

When you request your free Portfolio Stress Test, if you qualify, you are getting a free resource. There is no further obligation to do anything. There are NO hidden fees or costs of any kind when you receive your free Portfolio Stress Test.

Requesting your free Portfolio Stress Test is easy.

First, you'll need to visit www.FreePortfolioStressTest.com and request it.

Shortly after requesting your free Portfolio Stress Test, you will need to have a brief fifteen-minute conversation with one of our New Retirement Rules™ advisors so that he or she can get some basic information from you.

About one week after you provide this information, you will receive your Portfolio Stress Test from one of our New Retirement Rules™ advisors.

Let me tell you a bit about how the New Retirement Rules™ advisors work.

Our New Retirement Rules™ advisors charge fees to write financial plans using the "two bucket" approach. These written plans contain exact step-by-step instructions on how to set up and manage a "two bucket" approach for an individual's personal financial situation.

But not everyone qualifies to have a plan done for him or her. The ONLY circumstance under which a New Retirement

Rules™ advisor will write a plan for the client is when the fee to prepare the plan is significantly less than the savings identified by the plan. In other words, a client has to experience positive cash flow as a result of having this plan prepared. From our experience in designing plans, we know that many folks overpay on fees, taxes, and other financial expenses, and in many cases, a written plan can create positive cash flow for a client.

To be frank, there are many folks who receive a complete Portfolio Stress Test who aren't good fits to work with one of our New Retirement Rules™ advisors because positive cash flow could not be realized as a result of having the plan written.

If one of our New Retirement Rules™ advisors determines after preparing your Portfolio Stress Test that you could experience positive cash flow from the preparation of a plan, he or she will include your potential realized savings and the cost to prepare a plan for you.

Again, let me repeat: There is no obligation to hire an advisor to prepare a plan, and there is no cost for the Portfolio Stress Test.

We are sincere in our efforts to help folks understand the looming threats to their nest egg and genuine in our desire to help folks save money on taxes and other financial expenses on which many folks overpay.

Even if you don't qualify to benefit from a written plan, a Portfolio Stress Test can provide you with another viewpoint as to how best to manage your nest egg. At the very least, it will provide you with objective information to use when conversing with your present financial professional.

To request your free Portfolio Stress Test, simply visit www.FreePortfolioStressTest.com.

[1] This example is hypothetical and is not intended to illustrate any particular product.

[2] This illustration is hypothetical and for illustrative purposes only. A small change in illustrated assumptions could greatly alter the total tax paid.

Afterword

I sincerely hope this book has provided you with some perspectives you did not have prior to reading it.

A study of economic history concludes beyond any doubt that the current fiscal and economic policies being pursued around the world are not sustainable.

The end result of these policies is predictable, as Thomas Jefferson once stated:

If the American people ever allow private banks to control the issue of their currency, first by inflation, then by deflation, the banks and corporations that will grow up around them will deprive the people of all property until their children wake up homeless on the continent their fathers conquered.

In every prior economic winter season, there have been folks who have done quite well, and there have been folks who have had their nest eggs decimated. When reading any book like this one that offers a different but logical perspective, there is the temptation to simply "file away" that perspective and not take action.

I would urge you to not yield to that temptation. The stakes are high, and your retirement dreams might be on the line.

I wish you every success in not only protecting yourself from what lies ahead but also potentially prospering as well.

Made in the USA
Las Vegas, NV
08 November 2023

80485541R00090